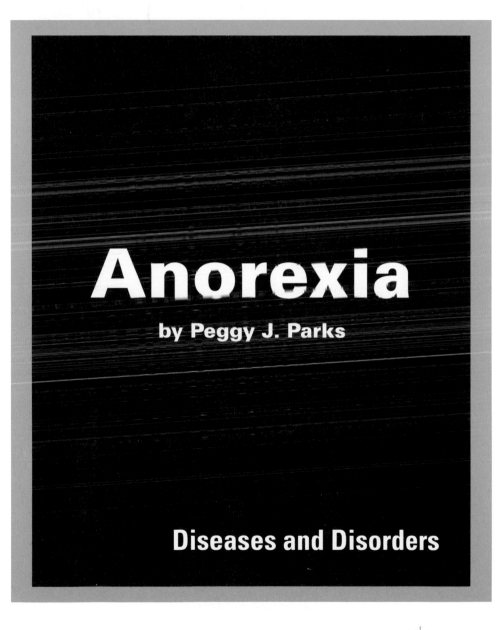

Anorexia

by Peggy J. Parks

Diseases and Disorders

ReferencePoint
Press™

San Diego, CA

wr

For more information, contact:
ReferencePoint Press, Inc.
PO Box 27779
San Diego, CA 92198
www.ReferencePointPress.com

Picture credits:
Maury Aaseng: 31–34, 49–53, 66–68, 82–84
AP Images: 11, 15

LIBRARY OF CONGRESS CATALOGING-IN-PUBLICATION DATA

Parks, Peggy J., 1951–
  Anorexia / by Peggy J. Parks.
    p. cm. — (Compact research)
  Includes bibliographical references and index.
  ISBN-13: 978-1-60152-042-5 (hardback)
  ISBN-10: 1-60152-042-5 (hardback)
  1. Anorexia nervosa—Popular works. I. Title.
  RC552.A5P37 2008
  616.85'262—dc22
                                                        2008004238

Contents

Foreword   4

Anorexia at a Glance   6

Overview   8

How Serious Is Anorexia?   19
    Primary Source Quotes   26
    Facts and Illustrations   30

What Causes Anorexia?   35
    Primary Source Quotes   43
    Facts and Illustrations   48

What Are the Health Risks of Anorexia?   54
    Primary Source Quotes   61
    Facts and Illustrations   65

Can Anorexia Be Cured?   69
    Primary Source Quotes   77
    Facts and Illustrations   81

Key People and Advocacy Groups   85

Chronology   88

Related Organizations   90

For Further Research   94

Source Notes   97

List of Illustrations   100

Index   101

About the Author   104

Foreword

Foreword

❝ Where is the knowledge we have lost in information? ❞

—"The Rock," T.S. Eliot.

As modern civilization continues to evolve, its ability to create, store, distribute, and access information expands exponentially. The explosion of information from all media continues to increase at a phenomenal rate. By 2020 some experts predict the worldwide information base will double every 73 days. While access to diverse sources of information and perspectives is paramount to any democratic society, information alone cannot help people gain knowledge and understanding. Information must be organized and presented clearly and succinctly in order to be understood. The challenge in the digital age becomes not the creation of information, but how best to sort, organize, enhance, and present information.

ReferencePoint Press developed the *Compact Research* series with this challenge of the information age in mind. More than any other subject area today, researching current issues can yield vast, diverse, and unqualified information that can be intimidating and overwhelming for even the most advanced and motivated researcher. The *Compact Research* series offers a compact, relevant, intelligent, and conveniently organized collection of information covering a variety of current topics ranging from illegal immigration and methamphetamine to diseases such as anorexia and meningitis.

The series focuses on three types of information: objective single-author narratives, opinion-based primary source quotations, and facts and statistics. The clearly written objective narratives provide context and reliable background information. Primary source quotes are carefully selected and cited, exposing the reader to differing points of view. And facts and statistics sections aid the reader in evaluating perspectives. Presenting these key types of information creates a richer, more balanced learning experience.

For better understanding and convenience, the series enhances information by organizing it into narrower topics and adding design features that make it easy for a reader to identify desired content. For example, in *Compact Research: Illegal Immigration*, a chapter covering the economic impact of illegal immigration has an objective narrative explaining the various ways the economy is impacted, a balanced section of numerous primary source quotes on the topic, followed by facts and full-color illustrations to encourage evaluation of contrasting perspectives.

The ancient Roman philosopher Lucius Annaeus Seneca wrote, "It is quality rather than quantity that matters." More than just a collection of content, the *Compact Research* series is simply committed to creating, finding, organizing, and presenting the most relevant and appropriate amount of information on a current topic in a user-friendly style that invites, intrigues, and fosters understanding.

Anorexia at a Glance

Prevalence

Anorexia is far more prevalent in Western countries than anywhere else in the world and affects an estimated 2.5 million people in the United States alone. More than 90 percent of anorexics are girls and young women. Males are also vulnerable to the disease, and the number of male anorexics is on the rise. Anorexia continues to diversify, affecting growing numbers of young children and adults, as well as minorities.

Cause

No one knows what causes anorexia, but researchers say it is a complex disease that involves a combination of biological, genetic, and environmental factors.

Bulimia Nervosa

Bulimia is not a starvation disease; rather, bulimics eat extraordinary amounts of food and then vomit to get rid of it after each meal. An estimated 50 percent of anorexics develop bulimia or bulimic patterns.

Symptoms

Anorexia symptoms typically happen in stages. Early symptoms include a refusal to eat, extreme weight loss, compulsive exercise, and personality changes such as moodiness and withdrawal. As starvation continues, more severe symptoms develop such as dry, brittle hair that falls out in clumps; pale, yellowish or gray skin; dark circles under the eyes; insomnia and fatigue; physical weakness; and low blood pressure, causing the anorexic to constantly feel cold.

Health Risks

Anorexia causes loss of critical bone mass, which can lead to crippling diseases such as osteoporosis, as well as anemia and other serious blood disorders. Severe malnourishment can cause electrolyte imbalance, which can be fatal. Hormonal changes include the cessation of menstruation in females and decreased testosterone in males. The greatest danger is that anorexia starves vital organs such as the heart, liver, and kidneys; this can cause organ failure and death.

Mortality Rate

Anorexia has the highest mortality rate of any other mental illness. An estimated 10 to 20 percent of people who have anorexia die from it, and risk of death among anorexics is as much as 12 times greater than for people of their same age who do not have the disease.

Treatment

Although there is no cure, many anorexics have recovered after being treated with a combination of medical care, psychotherapy, and nutrition counseling. Hospitalization has proven to have a high success rate, although eating disorder facilities are extremely expensive and the costs are often not covered by health insurance. Because anorexics are delusional and see themselves as fat even when their bodies are emaciated, recovering from the disease is often a lifelong process.

Overview

Overview

> **66** Anorexia is one of the deadliest psychiatric diseases; it's estimated that up to 15 percent of anorexics die, from suicide or complications related to starvation. **99**

—Harriet Brown, "One Spoonful at a Time."

> **66** Many times at parties women have made the joke, 'You know, I wish I could get just a little of that anorexia.' I always assure them that it only comes in one size— devastating. **99**

—Psychotherapist Steven Levenkron, *Anatomy of Anorexia.*

Anorexia nervosa, usually just called anorexia, is a serious mental health disease that involves compulsive dieting and drastic weight loss. According to the National Institute of Mental Health (NIMH), anorexia is characterized by "emaciation, a relentless pursuit of thinness and extremely disturbed eating behaviors, such as deliberate self-starvation."[1]

Anorexics (or anorectics) have such an intense fear of gaining weight that they can think of nothing else but being thin. Yet in spite of their self-starvation, they are obsessed with food—it is constantly on their minds, even to the point of keeping them awake at night. Recovered anorexic Stella Jones explains: "I would agonize over whether I'd eaten seven grapes or eight. I would stand in the kitchen for hours, trying to decide whether to allow myself food. . . . I'd wake up in a panic thinking I had eaten something I'd never let myself touch. I chewed food and spat it out in the sink just to taste it. I'd throw huge amounts of food in the trash."[2] As obsessed with food as anorexics are, they are convinced that if they give in to the desire to eat, they will become obese. If they indulge even the simplest craving, such as eating one small cookie, they are consumed with guilt and often exercise for hours to burn off the calories. Jones ran up to seven miles every day, even as she starved herself.

A Starvation Diet

Anorexics typically exist on fewer than 500 calories per day, while meticulously counting every single calorie they consume. Evelyn Strauss, who struggled with anorexia as a teenager, weighed cherries on a kitchen scale before eating them to make sure they were exactly 3.5 ounces (100 grams). Charlie Mileski, another recovered anorexic, knew that there were exactly 24 calories in licking a postage stamp. Lori Gottlieb was so obsessed with calories that she feared she would get fat from inhaling the steam from a casserole. "I figured the steam must be going right up my nose," she writes, "into my body, and straight to my stomach. I felt pretty full all of a sudden."[3] Former model and recovered anorexic Cleo Glyde once lived on a diet that consisted entirely of green grapes. She ate 3 grapes for breakfast and 2 for snacks. If she ate 6 grapes, she considered that to be binging. This is typical of the anorexic mentality: Food is considered the enemy.

> " Anorexics . . . have such an intense fear of gaining weight that they can think of nothing else but being thin. "

How Serious Is Anorexia?

Anorexia is a killer—it has the highest mortality rate of any mental illness. The disease affects an estimated 2.5 million people in the United States alone, and more than 90 percent of anorexics are girls and young women. The NIMH says that from .5 percent to 3.7 percent of females suffer from anorexia., although some studies show that it could be as high as 10 percent. Males, however, are also vulnerable to the disease, and the number of male anorexics is on the rise. Eating disorder specialists believe that there may be a higher prevalence of male anorexia than health care professionals know about, as the NIMH states: "Boys with eating disorders exhibit the same types of emotional, physical and behavioral signs and symptoms as girls, but for a variety of reasons, boys are less likely to be diagnosed with what is often considered a stereotypically 'female' disorder."[4]

In addition to gender diversification, anorexic victims are getting younger. In 2007, a 6-year-old boy from the United Kingdom was treated for anorexia. Surveys show that of hospital admissions in the UK during 2006, 51 boys and 36 girls under the age of 11 were suffering from the disease. The same is true in America, as eating disorder specialists say that more and more children are being admitted for treatment.

What Causes Anorexia?

Doctors still do not know exactly what causes anorexia, but they have a far better understanding of the disease than they did in the past. The old way of thinking was that anorexia was a conscious choice, something girls did to themselves in a relentless pursuit of thinness, or perhaps to look like celebrities featured in the media. Even health care professionals once considered it a frivolous disease, and they often blamed anorexics for intentionally harming themselves. This sort of viewpoint is rare today, but it does still exist. One young anorexic from the United Kingdom expresses her frustration at such a perspective because it minimizes the severity of the disease: "To think that people would actually really think that you would starve yourself to the point where you can barely stand up because you wanted to be a bit thinner and look like somebody who was on the television is quite insulting in a lot of ways."[5]

> Although it may seem unbelievable to those who do not understand anorexia, when anorexics look in the mirror, they see a fat person looking back at them.

Studies in recent years have shown that anorexia is far from frivolous, nor is it a disease of choice. It is now widely accepted that anorexia is a life-threatening disease that does not have one single cause; rather, a combination of different factors is involved, including genetics, personality type, hormones, and brain chemistry, as well as society and environment. Some particularly revealing studies have been conducted in twins, whereby researchers found that more than half a person's risk for developing the disease was determined by genetic factors.

"It's Like a Nightmare"

Although it may seem unbelievable to those who do not understand anorexia, when anorexics look in the mirror, they see a fat person looking back at them. The disease makes them delusional, completely distorting their sense of reality. Yet the thinner they become, the fatter they feel. Even if every ounce of body fat has melted off, anorexics look around and believe that everyone else is thinner than they are and no one can convince them they are wrong. Jessica Lyons went through this with a friend, and she explains how troubling the experience was: "It's like a nightmare where you see the boogeyman and you know it's going to kill her so you warn her, but she can't see it, so she doesn't believe you, and then she dies."[6]

At one point when author Marya Hornbacher was struggling with anorexia, she stood 5 feet 3 inches (160 cm) tall and weighed just 52 pounds (23.6 kg), yet she still saw herself as fat. The same was true with Aimee Liu; at 5 feet 7 inches (170 cm) and 98 pounds (44.5 kg), Liu was disgusted with what she perceived to be a fat body. She lived her life in terror of food and gaining weight, and often spent up to four hours a day bicycling, walking, and doing calisthenics. "I could clamp my knees together and slide a fist between my thighs with room to spare," she says. "Still, I berated myself in front of the mirror as I stepped on and off and on the scale. 'You are one fat slob.'"[7]

Ana Carolina Reston was on her way to becoming one of the world's top models. But she had a serious problem— she suffered from anorexia and lived on a meager diet of tomatoes and apples. At 5 feet 8 inches tall she weighed just 88 pounds. In November 2006, at the age of 21, Reston was dead.

Behavioral and Physical Symptoms

Anorexia can be recognized in a number of ways, depending on how far along the disease has progressed. Typically, the first symptom is someone's burning desire to become thinner, which results in obsessive dieting and compulsive exercise. As the anorexic continues to lose weight, he or she will likely be complimented by others who notice the weight loss and offer their praise, admiration, and envy. This gives the anorexic a sense of achievement, which breeds a determination to keep going, to restrict caloric intake further, and lose even more weight. As the pounds continue to drop off, anorexics can focus on nothing else but the compulsion to lose weight, which causes personality changes such as moodiness and social withdrawal. During meals, anorexics often make excuses for not eating, saying that they just do not feel hungry, as Stella Jones explains: "If I had to eat around other people, I'd spit food out in my napkin, or move it around on the plate, or invent stories explaining why I couldn't eat."[8] Ironically, though, it is not uncommon for people with anorexia to prepare elaborate gourmet meals for family and friends, often to prove to themselves that they do not need to eat it.

As anorexics continue to starve themselves, symptoms of their disease grow more severe. Their skin turns a sickly gray or yellow, and their hair becomes brittle and falls out. They may become defiant and angry, lashing out at family members and friends who confront them about needing to eat or to cut down on excessive exercise. They suffer from a near-constant state of fatigue and have trouble sleeping. Their blood pressure plummets, as does their body temperature, which causes them to feel constantly cold. It is not uncommon, even in very hot weather, for anorexics to bundle up in heavy sweaters and blankets and still be shaking uncontrollably. Lauren Sackey, who suffered from anorexia as a teenager, describes her experience with this: "After getting wet while jet skiing on a scorching summer day, I developed such an extreme chill that, despite a hot shower and layers of clothing, my body ached and shivered incessantly."[9] If the body temperature remains lower than normal, the body protects itself from hypothermia by growing a layer of fine, downy hair known as lanugo on the back, arms, and legs, and sometimes the face and neck.

Yet even as their bodies waste away, anorexics deny that anything is wrong with them, and often hide their emaciated bodies under layers of baggy clothes. They become severely depressed and withdrawn. Once they have reached this point, they are in serious danger of dying from the disease.

How Anorexics Harm Themselves

Because anorexics are obsessed with a never-ending quest for thinness, they often go to extreme measures to lose weight and keep it off. Along with self-starvation, many anorexics take laxatives, thinking that they can "wash foods out" of their bodies. Karen Schenk writes in *Women Today* magazine that during her struggle with anorexia, she took up to 60 laxatives a day. Anorexics also take diuretics to rid themselves of excess water, which causes dehydration and gives them the illusion that they weigh less than they actually do. Eventually, they lose so much weight that they are barely recognizable. Laura Penny, a recovered anorexic from the United Kingdom, describes the appearance of her roommate, Louise, when they shared a hospital room. "Louise is one of the sickest people I have ever met; at 23, she could pass for a 12-year-old were it not for her face, which is as withered and haunted as an old woman's."[10]

Many anorexics punish themselves for failing to achieve their thinness goals. They may viciously slash their wrists, arms, and legs with razor blades or other sharp objects. This was the case with Brittany Snow, an actress who starred in the movie *Hairspray*. Snow struggled with anorexia for nine years, and she says the more she could not control her eating, the more she cut herself. "I wanted to look at my wrist and be like, 'See what you did? You ate ____.' It wasn't about the food. It was an emotional problem. I wanted to bleed, but I didn't want to kill myself. It was about hurting myself so I could feel bad, cry and let it out."[11]

Bulimia Nervosa

Unlike anorexics who starve themselves, bulimics eat extraordinary amounts of food, often to the point of feeling so full that they are in physical pain. To counteract the effects of this binge eating, they force themselves to vomit. Another difference is that bulimics are not necessarily skinny; instead, their weight may fluctuate wildly, going from thin to overweight in a short period of time. Many have been known to eat 10 or more large meals a day, and vomit after each one. This causes severe dehydration, can harm the digestive system, and causes their throats to become chronically inflamed. Frequent vomiting can also destroy the teeth. When bulimics vomit repeatedly, hydrochloric acid from the stomach washes over teeth and erodes tooth enamel. Although enamel is one of the hardest substances on Earth, it cannot stand up to such a strong acid. As a result of chronic vomiting, the bulimic's teeth can literally melt away over time.

Although anorexia and bulimia are different types of diseases, it is common for people to cross over between them. About 50 percent of anorexics develop bulimia or bulimic patterns. One person who suffered from both diseases is Nalani Odi, a young woman who now lives in Hawaii. When Odi was teaching English in Japan, she became obsessed with her weight and drastically cut back on eating. As her body continued to grow thinner, she became so weak that she gasped for breath if she climbed just three steps on a staircase. "I've never been more unhealthy in my life," she says. "My body, as well as my life, fell apart."[12] Odi's friends begged her to start eating again, and although she tried, she found that she could not eat normally. That is when she went from anorexic to bulimic, and began a regular ritual of binging and purging.

> Although anorexia and bulimia are different types of diseases, it is common for people to cross over between them.

The Health Risks of Anorexia

Anorexia can have disastrous effects on physical health. The disease can wreak havoc on bones, causing damage that is often irreversible. When the body is starving, this causes a loss of bone mass—and once that bone mass is lost, it is often gone forever. This can lead to a painful, crippling bone disease called osteoporosis, which affects about 40 percent of anorexics.

Anorexia also causes serious hormonal changes, which can result in the stopping of menstruation. For younger anorexics, the first menstrual period is delayed and does not start until their body weight becomes normal. If menstruation has already begun, such as in teenagers and young women, starvation causes it to stop. Author Julia K. De Pree, who suffered with anorexia for many years, stopped menstruating during her struggle with the disease, as she explains: "My period disappeared along with my breasts and hips—signs of womanhood effaced by the compul-

Although there is no cure, many anorexics have recovered after being treated with a combination of medical care, psychotherapy, and nutrition counseling. This 25-year-old woman has a feeding tube surgically implanted in her stomach to assist with her caloric intake.

sion to starve. The body in disarray, the mind seeking to know the limit of physical form."[13]

The most deadly risk of anorexia is how it starves vital organs; when there is no longer any fat left for the body to burn for energy, it begins to digest itself. According to the Mayo Clinic, if anorexics become severely malnourished, "every organ in the body can sustain damage, including the brain, heart and kidneys. This damage may not be fully reversible, even when the anorexia is under control."[14] The heart is especially vulnerable to damage. As more and more weight is lost, the heart grows smaller and weaker. Heart damage is the most common reason for hospitalization in anorexics, and it is usually what kills them. In March 2006 a 20-year-old runner from Racine, Wisconsin, died from cardiac arrest related to anorexia. At the time of her death, Alex DeVinny was 5 feet 8 inches (182 cm) tall and weighed just 70 pounds (31.8 kg).

Pro-Ana Web Sites

One of the most disturbing trends among young anorexia sufferers is the proliferation of Web sites that actually promote the disease. These "pro-Ana" sites, as they are known to participants, started popping up on the Internet in 2000 and 2001. The sites promote the idea that anorexia is a lifestyle choice, and offer anorexics tips on issues such as how to suppress hunger, how to starve themselves, how to purge in the shower so no one can hear, and how to deceive parents and friends. There are also online photo galleries and videoclips, which are intended to provide "thinspiration" for anorexics, that feature ultraskinny celebrities. Dr. Susan Sawyer, who directs the eating disorder program at the Royal Children's Hospital in Melbourne, Australia, expresses her concern about such pro-Ana sites: "The fact that these websites are in such a detailed manner, giving people the weapons by which they can, in a sense, cause their own self-destruction is pretty tragic to watch."[15] Even though these sites are highly controversial, as well as potentially dangerous, they are legal because free speech on the Internet is protected under the First Amendment. But Internet providers have the right to shut sites down if they have legitimate reasons for doing so, such as violating terms of service. Under mounting pressure from eating disorder professionals and organizations, Yahoo!, Microsoft Network, and some other major Web hosts have begun policing sites and taking pro-Ana sites offline.

Can Anorexia Be Cured?

Because of its deep psychological roots, anorexia is one of the most difficult diseases to treat. To someone who is obsessed with not getting fat, the idea of gaining weight—even one or two pounds—is terrifying. No matter what anyone tells them, they remain convinced that they are too fat. Also, as anorexics get sicker, they become more desperate to deceive others by hiding their illness however they can. Diane Whiteoak, manager of a private hospital that treats eating disorders, explains: "Both anorexia nervosa and bulimia nervosa are very secretive conditions and in the majority of cases sufferers will avoid detection and actively resist treatment until they become very unwell and the illness is out of their control."[16]

Another reason anorexia treatment is challenging is that many people—including some health care professionals—still do not fully understand the disease or even take it seriously. Dr. Daniel le Grange, an eating disorder specialist from Chicago, says that even today, anorexia is often seen as something that patients bring on themselves. Families are also blamed, as writer Harriet Brown explains: "There are doctors and nurses in this community who still blame families when a child has an eating disorder. Who will tell you, with a look of disdain, that you did this to your child. You're the reason your child weighs 70 pounds and is too weak to sit up in bed. You're the reason your bright, charming, funny child can do nothing but shake and cry and still, even though she's starving to death, cannot eat."[17] Diane Brown, whose daughter Lauren suffered from anorexia from the age of 15, also encountered doctors who were not knowledgeable about the disease. One doctor examined Lauren and told her there was nothing wrong—he said that Diane and her husband were the problem. Over the following years, Lauren became so emaciated that her parents could hardly bear to look at her. Eventually, the disease claimed her life. In August 2003, Lauren died in her sleep at the age of 25.

Treatment for anorexia often includes a combination of medical care, psychotherapy, nutrition counseling, and in many cases, hospitalization. But only about 1 out of 10 people who suffer from anorexia ever get treated for it. This is largely because such treatment is extremely expensive—ranging from $500 to $2,000 per day, with the average cost for a month of hospitalization about $30,000. These costs are often not covered by health insurance.

Is There Hope for Anorexics?

Fortunately, anorexia awareness and treatment have improved as more health care professionals have gained a better understanding of the disease.

Research continues to broaden their knowledge and insight. Also, increasing numbers of anorexics are speaking out about their disease, as are families who have lost a loved one to anorexia. People are beginning to talk more about prevention and be aware of early symptoms in an effort to head off the disease before it strikes. Eating disorder specialist Cynthia Bulik makes it clear that it is critical for parents to educate themselves about anorexia and learn to watch for possible symptoms, as she explains: "If your child comes to you and they're a normal weight and they say they're going on a diet, you should take that as seriously as if your child was to say, 'Mom, I'm going to have my first cigarette today,' or 'I'm going to have a beer with dinner tonight.' The red flags need to go up."[18]

> **With continued advancements in anorexia treatment, eating disorder specialists are hopeful that the survival rate will improve—but this is something they just do not know. Even anorexics who have recovered live their whole lives not knowing if they will ever be truly free of the disease.**

With continued advancements in anorexia treatment, eating disorder specialists are hopeful that the survival rate will improve—but this is something they just do not know. Even anorexics who have recovered live their whole lives not knowing if they will ever be truly free of the disease. De Pree is one of them. Although her struggle with anorexia happened years ago, she still sometimes feels afraid and unsure: "There are aspects of this insidious illness that have never left me, may not ever leave," she writes. "I have learned to understand some of this."[19]

How Serious Is Anorexia?

66Anorexia is a killer—it has the highest mortality rate of any mental illness, including depression.99

—Peg Tyre, "Fighting Anorexia: No One to Blame."

66Seeing your child commit slow suicide in front of you by denying herself food, and actually watching her body disappear, is the worst torture in the world.99

—Jacqui Flicker, quoted in Amanda Cable, "My Little Girl, Anorexic at 12."

Ana Carolina Reston was on her way to becoming one of the world's top models. The Brazilian beauty had modeled in China, Turkey, Mexico, and Japan, and looked forward to a successful career. But Reston had a serious problem—she suffered from anorexia and lived on a meager diet of tomatoes and apples. Her mother watched as she continued to lose weight, and tried to convince her daughter to seek help. Reston, however, insisted she was fine, that there was nothing wrong, even though at 5 feet 8 inches (182 cm) tall she weighed just 88 pounds (40 kg). Then in October 2006, she complained of pain in her kidneys and was admitted to a hospital in San Paolo, Brazil. Her body was emaciated, her face gaunt, her skin colorless, and her once thick, lustrous hair was dry and brittle, with clumps having fallen out. Less than a month later, at the age of 21, Reston was dead. Her family and friends were devastated, as her mother expressed: "I didn't know what my daughter had could kill, but I knew it had to be treated. But my daughter rejected me, she said she was OK. . . . I don't know how I'm supposed to survive now."[20]

"Epidemic Proportions"

Prior to the 1980s, there was little awareness of the disease called anorexia nervosa. It was not even classified as a psychiatric disorder until the third edition of the *Diagnostic and Statistical Manual of Mental Disorders* was published in 1980. Even many health care professionals were not familiar with anorexia, nor did they have any idea how to treat it. Then in 1983, when the popular singer Karen Carpenter died of heart failure caused by anorexia, the disease was thrust into the public eye. Today, eating disorder specialists understand a great deal more than was known in the past, and they are aware that anorexia is a deadly disease—one that is becoming more prevalent all the time, as New York psychotherapist Steven Levenkron explains: "Anorexia was once a rare, or rarely reported, disorder. For the past twenty years, it has assumed epidemic proportions and shows no signs of quitting."[21]

The statistics related to anorexia are sobering. A study by the National Association of Anorexia Nervosa and Associated Disorders showed that 5 to 10 percent of anorexics die within 10 years after contracting the disease; 18 to 20 percent of anorexics will be dead after 20 years; and only 30 to 40 percent ever fully recover. "The mortality rate for anorexia nervosa is higher than that of any other psychiatric disorder," says psychiatrist Walter Kaye, "and it is the leading cause of death in young women."[22]

The Changing Face of Anorexia

Years ago, anorexia was thought to be a malady that afflicted privileged, attention-seeking white girls. In her 1978 book, *The Golden Cage: The Enigma of Anorexia Nervosa*, author Hilde Bruch, MD, captured this perspective: "New diseases are rare, and a disease that selectively befalls the young, rich, and beautiful is practically unheard of. But such a disease is affecting the daughters of well-to-do, educated, and successful families. . . . The chief symptom is severe starvation leading to a devastating weight loss; 'she looks like the victim of a concentration camp' is a not uncommon description."[23]

Bruch's description still applies to many anorexia sufferers, but no longer is the disease so narrowly confined to one particular age and sociocultural group. In recent years, psychotherapists and other health care professionals have begun to see much more diversity among patients diagnosed with anorexia. One glaring difference is age. Although anorexia is a disease that typically affects teenagers, eating disorder specialists are seeing increasing numbers of patients who are in their 30s, 40s, 50s, and even older. Psychiatrists Mori J. Krantz and Philip S. Mehler wrote an article in July 2004 about one of their patients, a 52-year-old woman who had a long history with anorexia. At the time she was hospitalized, she had lost a massive amount of weight and was suffering from severe pain in her legs, weakness, and fatigue. Indicative of the seriousness of her disease was the growth of furry lanugo that covered her face and arms.

On the opposite end of the spectrum, anorexics are also getting younger. Eating disorder specialists report an alarming spike in the number of children diagnosed with anorexia. Dr. Dee Dawson, who is the founder and medical director at Rhodes Farm eating disorder clinic in London, says that the ages of patients suffering from anorexia are decreasing all the time. The clinic treats girls as young as 8 or 9, and one patient was just 6 years old. Dr. David S. Rosen, who is an eating disorder specialist at the University of Michigan Medical School, says that back in 2000 "the idea of seeing a 9- or 10-year-old anorexic would have been shocking. . . . Now we're seeing kids this age all the time."[24] He adds that there is no explanation for why the number of child anorexics is growing, but it could be related to increased awareness among parents about the symptoms of eating disorders.

> " Years ago, anorexia was thought to be a malady that afflicted privileged, attention-seeking white girls. "

Kennedy Pieken, a little girl from Iowa, began her battle with anorexia when she was just four years old. When asked why she suddenly stopped eating, she replied: "I don't know. Because my brain was telling me not to eat."[25] Kennedy screamed when her mother tried to force a bit of peach in her mouth, and during mealtimes, she pretended to eat by taking tiny bites and holding food in her cheeks so she could spit it out later.

The race of anorexics is also diversifying. For years it was almost exclusively a disease of white people, but that has begun to change. While no exact figures exist for how many African Americans, Asians, and Hispanics suffer from anorexia, eating disorder specialists say the number is on the rise. According to Dr. Gayle Brooks, a psychologist who specializes in eating disorders, anorexia did not traditionally affect women of color because their cultures were more accepting of different body sizes; as a result, they felt less pressure to be thin. She explains: "Curvy African-American women were celebrated. These girls didn't experience anxiety and shame about their bodies. Being curvy or large was a source of pride within the African-American community."[26] Now, though, Brooks and her colleagues are noticing a trend of more severe eating disorders among African American girls. In July 2001, Kaelyn Carson, a 20-year-old black college sophomore from Michigan, died of a heart attack related to a lengthy battle with anorexia. She had been a college track star and an honors student and had won the title of Miss Michigan American Teen—but at the time of her death, she weighed only 79 pounds (35.8 kg).

Anorexic Males

Once a decidedly female disease, anorexia now afflicts growing numbers of boys and men. A February 2007 survey by researchers from Harvard University showed that males represented as many as one-quarter of anorexia patients. No one knows for sure whether the number of male patients with eating disorders is actually increasing, or if more men and boys are now speaking out about their disease and seeking treatment. Studies have shown that male anorexics have a higher risk for early death than females, which may be because they either are not diagnosed at all, or are diagnosed later in life than girls and women.

> "Once a decidedly female disease, anorexia now afflicts growing numbers of boys and men."

One young man who suffered from anorexia during his teenage years is Daniel Johns, the lead singer of the rock band Silverchair. Johns, who at his lowest weight was just 110 pounds (50 kg), nearly died from the disease. When he was at his worst, he could not stand the look, smell, or taste of food; and if anyone talked about eating, he would leave the room. Finally, when doctors convinced him that he was going to die, he entered a treatment program. Although he has recovered, a likely result of the disease is a painful case of arthritis, as he explains: "The arthritis just went from bad to worse and went through all the bones in my body, through my spine, up into my neck. I just couldn't move. . . . I couldn't have a shower because it felt like I was cracking my spine."[27]

"I Just Wanted All the Fat Gone"

Anorexia is an insidious disease—one that crowds out reality and fills the mind with delusional thoughts. Some anorexics say it feels like a demon is inside them, controlling their every move. Even if they are weak with hunger, they hear voices in their heads chastising them, telling them that they have no business eating food, or do not deserve to eat. Grace Bowman, a recovered anorexic from the United Kingdom, said she heard such a voice 24 hours a day, 7 days a week, and she could not silence it. It told her she was not good enough, that she was not thin enough, that she needed to keep dieting, that she needed to keep getting smaller. This also happened to Evelyn Strauss when she was struggling with anorexia, and she describes how powerful of a force it was: "Eventually I was no longer directing my diet; it was directing me. 'Don't eat that,' I'd hear as I lifted the smaller half of an English muffin to my mouth. 'Don't nourish yourself,' a voice bellowed, stilling the edge of my spoon a mere millimeter into a cantaloupe's flesh."[28]

Anorexics lose the ability to see themselves as they really are, and they despise the image that they believe they see in the mirror. Their families and friends watch their bodies wasting away, and beg them to stop starving themselves. Yet anorexics cannot see what others see; they never stop believing that they are fat and are convinced that everyone around them is skinnier. Bria Roberts, who was so emaciated and sick that she had to be hospitalized and force-fed, describes how this delusion affected her: "I actually would grab parts of my body and I would just sit there wishing I could cut that part off. I just wanted all the fat gone and every time I looked, I saw fat, even though everybody was telling me I was so small."[29]

Margaret Donlevy is also familiar with what delusion can do to an anorexic. Her 14-year-old granddaughter, Nicole, had been a happy,

> **Anorexics cannot see what others see; they never stop believing that they are fat and are convinced that everyone around them is skinnier.**

healthy teenage girl. Then in January 2006, she suddenly became terrified at the notion of being fat and stopped eating. Her weight began to drop and her personality radically changed, as Donlevy explains: "We had a happy, smiley, liked-drama-and-dancing kind of girl before. Now it is as if she has been replaced by a stranger; a sad, depressed, frightened stranger who shows no emotion unless it concerns her battle with food."[30] Doctors diagnosed anorexia, but because there are no eating disorder clinics in the part of Scotland where Nicole lives, she was admitted to a psychiatric facility in Edinburgh. In an April 2007 article, Donlevy stated that Nicole had not improved, her weight was still dangerously low, and no one could say for sure whether she would recover.

Self-Destruction as Punishment

Anorexics harm themselves in many different ways. The very nature of their disease is harmful because of how it destroys the body. But many also cause intentional harm by slashing their arms and legs with razors or other sharp instruments. Anorexia sufferers do not do this in an effort to commit suicide; rather, they are trying to punish themselves for what they perceive to be total failure to control their eating. People who cut their bodies in this way are often called "cutters." After starving herself for more than a year, a young anorexic named Eleena began cutting herself when she started to gain weight: "I was just so ashamed of my body," she says. "I felt like I was the biggest failure and the weakest person . . . I remember picking up a knife from the kitchen and starting to cut myself on my arms, on my legs. I had so much pain inside of me, and so much hatred and animosity towards myself, that feeling the pain and making it real pain . . . it was calming. I did that for a long time."[31]

> Many [anorexics] cause intentional harm by slashing their arms and legs with razors or other sharp instruments.

Lauren Simmons (not her real name) vividly remembers the time she saw what a cutter had done to herself. Simmons worked for a psychiatrist who saw many females with eating disorders, but one stood out from the rest. She explains:

This particular patient, we'll call her "Chloe," was about 20 years old and came in once a week for therapy. She had been hospitalized on several occasions but didn't seem to be making much progress, as she was very, very sick. The doctor explained that it was difficult to cure Chloe because she thought she was fat, which blew me away because this girl was about 5'9" (175 cm) tall and weighed maybe 90 pounds (41 kg). She always wore long, loose-fitting pants and long-sleeved shirts so I never actually saw how thin she was. Then one hot summer day she came in for a session wearing short-shorts and a tank top, and I was shocked— not only because of her skeleton-like body, but also because her arms and legs were covered with ugly, jagged scars. They were everywhere, as though she had been brutally slashed over and over again with a razor-sharp knife. In my entire lifetime, I had never seen anything so horrid. Later I asked the doctor if she had been in some kind of tragic accident and he said no, that she had done it to herself. She was a cutter, someone who was so filled with self-loathing that she could not stop punishing herself. I have never forgotten that day, and I doubt that I ever will.[32]

Uncertainty Lingers

No longer is there any doubt that anorexia is a serious, life-threatening disease. Research clearly shows that it is; it also shows that the number of anorexia sufferers is on the rise and the people afflicted by it are of diverse genders, races, and ages. The ongoing uncertainty is whether health care professionals will find ways to break through the walls of delusion and help anorexics face the truth about what they are doing to themselves— because only then will they have a chance to get better.

How Serious Is Anorexia?

❝I tried to kill myself, through a slow and painful process called starvation.❞

> —Louise, quoted in "Dying to Be Thin: Share Your Story," PBS *NOVA*, December 12, 2000. www.pbs.org.

Louise is a young woman from Connecticut who struggled with anorexia for six years and finally regained her health.

❝Anorexia and bulimia affect ten million adult women and one million men in the United States.❞

> —Ilyse Simon, "The Body Battle," *Healthy Living Magazine*, Fall 2006/Winter 2007. www.hvhealthyliving.com.

Simon is a nutritionist who specializes in eating disorders.

* Editor's Note: While the definition of a primary source can be narrowly or broadly defined, for the purposes of Compact Research, a primary source consists of: 1) results of original research presented by an organization or researcher; 2) eyewitness accounts of events, personal experience, or work experience; 3) first-person editorials offering pundits' opinions; 4) government officials presenting political plans and/or policies; 5) representatives of organizations presenting testimony or policy.

❝The age of children suffering eating disorders is definitely getting younger and younger; there is no doubt about that at all.❞

—Dr. Dee Dawson, quoted in Amelia Hill, "Miranda Almost Died from Anorexia. She Is Eight Years Old," *The Observer*, November 18, 2007. www.guardian.co.uk.

Dawson is the founder and medical director of Rhodes Farm, Great Britain's first and largest residential clinic for child anorexics.

❝There are times I feel like I am drowning in my fear, sorrow, depression—and I find it hard to climb out and get on with life.❞

—Anonymous, quoted in "Dying to Be Thin: Share Your Story," PBS *NOVA*, December 12, 2000. www.pbs.org.

This is an anonymous quote from the PBS *NOVA* documentary "Dying to Be Thin: Share Your Story."

❝Eating disorders are not due to a failure of will or behavior; rather, they are real, treatable medical illnesses in which certain maladaptive patterns of eating take on a life of their own.❞

—National Institute of Mental Health (NIMH), "Eating Disorders: Facts About Eating Disorders and the Search for Solutions," August 24, 2007. www.nimh.nih.gov.

NIMH is the largest scientific organization in the world dedicated to the understanding, treatment, and prevention of mental disorders, including eating disorders.

66I would stretch a cookie for a month by eating it in crumbs, dissect Brussels sprouts one leaf at a time, sip a spoonful of yogurt as if it were scalding soup.99

—Aimee Liu, *Gaining: The Truth About Life After Eating Disorders.* New York: Warner Books, 2007, p. xii.

Liu is an author who struggled with anorexia for much of her life before overcoming the illness and going on to help others with eating disorders.

66Eating disorder associations say that about 86 percent of the approximately 10 million American girls and women—and one million boys and men—who suffer from an eating disorder reported the onset of their condition by [age] 20.99

—Alex Williams, "Before Spring Break, the Anorexic Challenge," *The New York Times*, April 2, 2006. www.nytimes.com.

Williams is a writer for *The New York Times.*

66Very often it is someone with self-esteem issues who believes *'if only I were thin* . . . then everything would be better.' Once they start losing weight, it doesn't satisfy them.99

—Dr. Amy Blumberg, quoted in "The Body Battle," *Healthy Living Magazine*, Fall 2006/Winter 2007. www.hvhealthyliving.com.

Blumberg is a psychotherapist who works with eating disorder patients in Poughkeepsie, New York.

66 Anorexia and its behaviors—eating rituals, lying, hiding from friends and relatives—can easily take over a patient's existence, and it's often easier for patients to live with the disease than face the factors that contribute to it. 99

—Peggy O'Farrell, "UC Student Overcoming Anorexia," *The Cincinnati Enquirer*, July 27, 2003. www.enquirer.com.

O'Farrell is a staff writer with *The Cincinnati Enquirer*.

66 An eating disorder is distorted thinking. An anorexic perceives herself larger than she is, and that's a distorted perception of reality. 99

—Dr. Theresa Yonker, quoted in Ilyse Simon, "The Body Battle," *Healthy Living*, Fall 2006/Winter 2007, www.hvhealthyliving.com.

Yonker is a holistic psychiatrist in Red Hook, New York.

66 If you're a mother of girls and you diet all the time, it's pretty hard to tell your daughter to be satisfied with her own appearance. 99

—Dr. Dave Rosen, quoted in Carl Jackson, "Eating Disorders," *Healthy Children*, Fall 2007. www.aap.org.

Rosen is an eating disorder specialist at the University of Michigan Medical School.

How Serious Is Anorexia?

- Anorexia has the **highest mortality rate** of any mental illness.

- The mortality rate associated with anorexia nervosa is **12 times** higher than the death rate of all causes of death for females 15 to 24 years old.

- Anorexia affects an estimated **2.5 million** people in America.

- Anorexia is much more prevalent in **Western countries**, although in some non-Western countries the disease is on the rise.

- More than **90 percent** of anorexics are girls and young women.

- About **1 in 200** American women suffers from anorexia.

- An estimated **95 percent** of those who have eating disorders are between the ages of 12 and 25.

- According to the National Institute of Mental Health, **nearly 4 percent** of females will have anorexia at some point during their lifetimes.

- About **50 percent** of anorexics develop bulimia or bulimic patterns.

- After asthma and obesity, anorexia is the **third most common** chronic illness among adolescent females.

Anorexia Develops at a Young Age

Although anorexia effects people of all ages, the the greatest number of anorexics are between 11 and 20 years old. As the pie chart illustrates, 76 percent of anorexia onset occurs by age 20. Only 14 percent of anorexics develop the disease after age 20.

Age at Onset of Anorexia

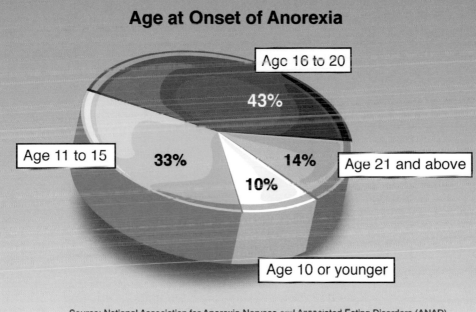

Age 16 to 20

43%

Age 11 to 15   33%   14%   Age 21 and above

10%

Age 10 or younger

Source: National Association for Anorexia Nervosa and Associated Eating Disorders (ANAD), "Facts About Eating Disorders." www.anad.org.

- Anorexia and bulimia affect as many as **10 million** females and **1 million** males in the United States.

- Anorexia is estimated to affect from **0.5 to 3 percent** of all teenagers.

- Over the past 40 years, incidence of anorexia in young women **has tripled**, while the number of teenagers with the disease has remained unchanged.

- Approximately **40 percent** of newly identified cases of anorexia are in girls 15 to 19 years old.

Symptoms and Signs of Anorexia

People who suffer from anorexia display a number of symptoms and signs, depending on the severity of their disease and how far along it has progressed. The following chart shows some of the most common symptoms and signs; as the anorexic becomes sicker, symptoms grow more severe and life threatening.

- **Obesession with food, extremely low-calorie diet, weight loss**
- **Excuses for not eating; moving food around on plates; cooking elaborate meals for other people without eating**
- **Compulsive exercise**
- **Wearing baggy clothes to conceal wasting body**
- **Irritability, moodiness, withdrawal from family and friends; denial of disease**
- **Near-constant fatigue; insomnia**
- **Skin turns a sickly gray or yellowish pallor**
- **Hair becomes dry and brittle, falls out in clumps**
- **A drop in blood pressure and body temperature, causing feelings of constantly being cold**
- **Fine, downy hair (lanugo) grows on the back, arms, legs, face, and neck**
- **Severe depression and suicidal remarks, such as the wish to die rather than live in such pain**

Sources: Duke University Student Health Center, "Eating Disorders Comparison Chart," 2005. http://healthydevil.student affairs.duke.edu; Steven Levenkron, *Anatomy of Anorexia*. New York: W.W. Norton & Company, 2000.

- Anorexics typically lose from **15 to 60 percent** of normal body fat.

- The risk of death by suicide among anorexics is estimated to be more than **50 times** higher than that of healthy women.

- When anorexia occurs in young adults, males are **more likely** to conceal it than females.

- **Substance abuse** is common among anorexics.

- According to the National Association of Anorexia Nervosa and Associated Disorders, an estimated **11 percent** of high school students have been diagnosed with an eating disorder.

- The CDC reports that **4.5 percent** of students in American schools have vomited or taken laxatives to lose weight or to keep from gaining weight.

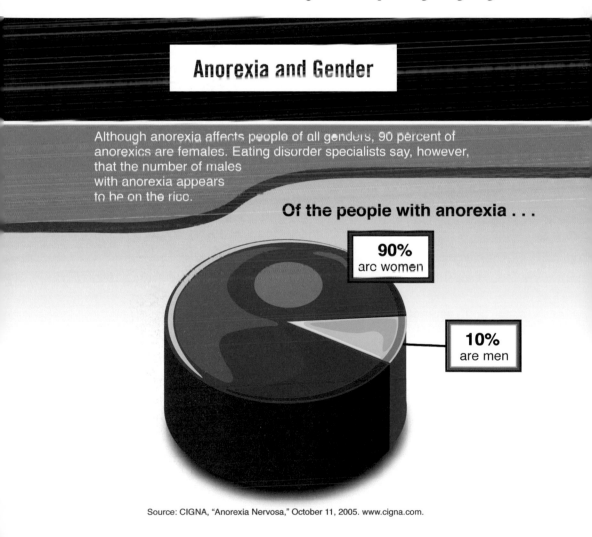

Anorexia and Gender

Although anorexia affects people of all genders, 90 percent of anorexics are females. Eating disorder specialists say, however, that the number of males with anorexia appears to be on the rise.

Of the people with anorexia . . .

90%
are women

10%
are men

Source: CIGNA, "Anorexia Nervosa," October 11, 2005. www.cigna.com.

The Disease of Delusion

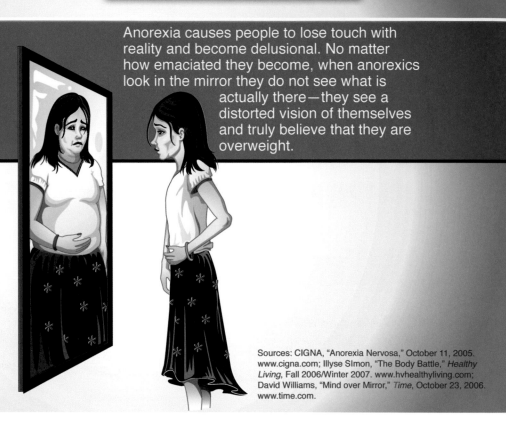

Anorexia causes people to lose touch with reality and become delusional. No matter how emaciated they become, when anorexics look in the mirror they do not see what is actually there—they see a distorted vision of themselves and truly believe that they are overweight.

Sources: CIGNA, "Anorexia Nervosa," October 11, 2005. www.cigna.com; Illyse Simon, "The Body Battle," *Healthy Living*, Fall 2006/Winter 2007. www.hvhealthyliving.com; David Williams, "Mind over Mirror," *Time*, October 23, 2006. www.time.com.

- According to the National Eating Disorders Association, **35 percent** of "normal dieters" progress to pathological dieting; of those, as many as **25 percent** develop eating disorders.

- Eating disorders are one of the most common psychological problems suffered by young women in Japan; but because seeking treatment is considered **shameful**, many go undiagnosed.

What Causes Anorexia?

66 There is a high public awareness of anorexia. But often it's seen as something you have brought down on yourself. You wouldn't tell a child who has cancer to just snap out of it.99

—Daniel le Grange, PhD, quoted in Marcia Froelke Coburn, "When Girls Won't Eat."

66 While the symptoms are behavioral, this illness has a biological core, with genetic components.99

—Lynn Grefe, quoted in Tina Kelley, "Insurer Sued for Refusing to Pay Costs of Anorexia."

The cause of anorexia has been a subject of controversy for many years. Not so long ago, the primary blame was placed on how society scorns fat and values thinness; people believed that girls intentionally starved themselves because they wanted skinnier bodies. Anorexia was also trivialized, even glamorized, as though the word *anorexic* were nothing more than a synonym for *thin*. In 1999, a billboard appeared in Sioux Falls, South Dakota, featuring a full-color photograph of the three female stars of the hit television show *Friends*. The copy that accompanied the photo read, "Cute anorexic chicks." Fortunately, people are starting to understand that nothing is trivial nor glamorous about anorexia, nor can it solely be caused by the media and society. Although anorexia's cause is still a mystery, it is widely believed to be a serious mental disorder that has roots in a complex combination of genetics and brain chemistry. Harriet Brown writes that, "most eating-disorders researchers have begun to think that there is no single cause of anorexia, that maybe it's more like a recipe, where several ingredients—genetics, personality type, hormones, stressful life events—come together in just the wrong way."[33]

Inside the Mind of an Anorexic

While no two anorexia sufferers are necessarily the same, researchers have identified similarities. One characteristic that is typically shared by anorexics is extreme perfectionism. They are constantly concerned with doing things right; they maintain high standards for themselves, want to please people, and crave exactness and order in their lives. Aimee Liu, who struggled with anorexia for many years, says that perfectionism is a consistent trait among anorexics. She explains: "Most people who have had an eating disorder believe down to their nerve endings that perfection is a real, attainable noble state and that it is their right and duty to claim it, whether they are performing in a play, organizing a closet, planning a party, or anticipating a date. They probably can't tell you why they feel this way, but the ultimate standard nevertheless shadows them like a malevolent conscience."[34]

> " One characteristic that is typically shared by anorexics is extreme perfectionism. "

Psychotherapist Steven Levenkron agrees that perfectionism is a common trait among anorexics. He adds, though, that the perfection they try to attain is much more obsessive than that of competitive athletes, musicians, artists, and others who strive for perfection in their craft. Unlike people who have a healthy attitude about achievements, anorexics never feel that they have accomplished their thinness goal. "A person has an obsessional disorder," says Levenkron, "when his or her goal, the methods used toward obtaining that goal, and the constant repetition of those methods become one never-ending process and the pursuit has no finish line . . . whereas the addictive personality can get high enough or drunk enough, the obsessional personality will never 'get there.' There is no 'fix' for an obsession."[35]

"Why I Won't Eat"

Health care professionals who specialize in eating disorders often find that anorexics are generally unhappy people. This proved to be a commonality among 15 chronic anorexia sufferers from the United Kingdom who participated in an in-depth study. The research, entitled "Why I Won't Eat," was published in the 2006 issue of *Journal of Health Psychology.* Part of it reads: "The major issue to emerge from all of our interviews was that something had gone wrong in the lives of these anorexic patients. . . . All of the patients in the sample were unhappy."[36] The authors add that many of the patients used self-starvation as a way of filling the void that unhappiness left. As harmful as anorexia was to their bodies, the disease allowed them to feel a sense of satisfaction because they were finally able to take control of something. "By exercising control over food, patients felt they were somehow offsetting potential disaster in other areas of their lives."[37]

This desire for control is very common among anorexia sufferers. Anorexics typically say they are proud of their ability to assume control of their food intake. Even if they feel like failures at everything else in their lives, whether they eat or not is completely within their control. Erika Goodman, an anorexia sufferer who was formerly a ballerina with the Joffrey Ballet, described this on the PBS television documentary *Dying to Be Thin:* "Because other things in your life aren't working, and [starving is] the one thing you have control over. And that's a major thing. I think that's what keeps a lot of these people in this anorexic mode. It's control. Nobody else can control that for you."[38]

Brain Studies with Anorexics

The more researchers study anorexia, the more they become convinced that the disease has biological roots. Cynthia Bulik says that for people with certain wiring, "biology takes on a life of its own. The train just starts running."[39]

Researchers are finding important differences in the brain chemistry of anorexics. A research team from the University of Pittsburgh, led by Dr. Walter Kaye, performed studies with former anorexic patients and discovered unusually high levels of a chemical called serotonin in their brains. Although serotonin is typically connected with feelings of well-being, excessive levels are linked to a sense of perpetual anxiety and obsessional thinking. According to Kaye, this could mean that dieting—even to the point of starvation—might be an unconscious way for anorexia sufferers to lower their serotonin levels to reduce anxiety. "This may explain the vicious cycle that people with anorexia get in," he says. "They have too much serotonin. They starve themselves. That drives down the serotonin." Kaye adds that the brain naturally adapts to depleted serotonin levels by producing more serotonin. "So people have to keep starving themselves more and more to reduce the serotonin, but the receptors keep up regulating. So they can never really escape from it."[40]

> " Researchers are finding important differences in the brain chemistry of anorexics. "

Kaye has conducted other brain research with anorexics, such as one study that appeared in the December 2007 *American Journal of Psychiatry.* The study involved two groups of women: one composed of recovered anorexics and the other of healthy people who had never suffered from anorexia. The two groups were asked to play a computer game and were told that they would be rewarded for correct guesses. During the test, researchers used functional magnetic resonance imaging (MRI) scans to monitor the women's brain activity. They found that the two groups' brains performed differently while they were playing the game. Among the nonsufferers, the part of the brain connected to emotional responses showed strong differences when the women were winning or losing. This was not the case with the group of former anorexics, however. Their MRI scans showed little difference in brain activity whether they won or lost the game, which led the researchers to suspect that the women got no more pleasure from winning than they did from losing. Kaye later discussed what he believes the findings meant: "This piece of research points to the fact that the brains of people with anorexia are wired differently . . . they react and think in different ways to the ordinary person and that they are more likely to go on to develop anorexia. . . . Deep down in their brain there appear to be biological differences that don't go away."[41]

Is Anorexia Genetic?

Eating disorder specialists and other health care professionals have long wondered about the possibility of anorexia being hereditary, in the same way that schizophrenia, depression, and other diseases run in families. There have been numerous studies to determine whether anorexia has genetic roots, and many researchers are now convinced that it does. According to Craig Johnson, president of the National Eating Disorders Association, if someone has a family member who has had anorexia, he or she is 12 times more at risk of developing the disease. Thus far, researchers have not located a particular gene that causes anorexia, but they believe there is definitely a genetic link.

Many researchers have sought to prove the relationship between genes and anorexia by studying twins. In one such study, which was made public in March 2006, researchers at the University of North Carolina at Chapel Hill and the Karolinska Institute in Stockholm, Sweden, analyzed a registry of more than 31,000 twins. After a statistical analysis, the researchers found that anorexia was far more prevalent among identical twins. They determined that 56 percent of someone's chances for developing anorexia was due to genetics.

Genetic research with twins has also resulted in interesting findings about anorexia in males. It has long been known that anorexia affects far more females than males, yet no one knows why. A study that was published in the December 2007 issue of *Archives of General Psychiatry* offered a possible reason. It showed that prenatal exposure to certain female hormones in the womb could increase someone's risk of developing anorexia later in life. After analyzing 4,478 pairs of opposite-sex twins, the researchers found that males with a twin sister had a significantly higher risk of developing the disease when compared with other males, and they also had the same chance of becoming anorexic as their sisters. Dr. Marco Procopio, a psychiatrist who co-authored the study, offers his interpretation of the findings: "This study shows the importance of the intrauterine environment in the development of anorexia. Possibly there is a need for genetic predisposition and a certain hormonal environment in utero to develop the illness."[42]

Anorexia and Environment

Eating disorder specialists are well aware that no one "catches" anorexia as though it were a virus, nor can environment alone cause someone to be anorexic. Much like having a predisposition for clinical depression or alcoholism, some people are naturally vulnerable to developing anorexia at some point in their lives. Yet the importance of environment cannot be downplayed, as it is a powerful influence, especially on impressionable children and teenagers. For someone who has the right mix of biological traits, anorexia can be set off by environmental factors such as trauma, grief, family problems, or sexual abuse. As Johnson explains: "Genetics loads the gun. Environment pulls the trigger."[43]

> " Eating disorder specialists are well aware that no one "catches" anorexia as though it were a virus, nor can environment alone cause someone to be anorexic. "

One environmental factor that sometimes triggers the onset of anorexia is bullying and teasing by schoolmates. When Charles Johnson was a seventh grader at a middle school in Pennsylvania, he was a little overweight for his age. One day he walked into gym class and everyone started calling him fat and throwing things at him. He was hurt and embarrassed, and ran away, vowing to himself that he would lose weight. He began eating a healthier diet and running almost every day, and by the end of six months, the same kids who had teased him were telling him he looked great. He enjoyed the compliments but before long, he found that he was becoming obsessed with food. Even though he had lost the excess weight, he never got over the fear of being fat or the mortification of being teased. "I wasn't chubby anymore," he says, "but I was so worried about being the 'chubby kid' I used to be that no matter what my body looked like, I wasn't satisfied."[44] He continued losing weight until, on his eighteenth birthday, his mother confronted him about his eating disorder and insisted that he get treatment. At the time he was terrified, but now he knows that it saved his life.

How much of an impact families have on someone developing anorexia is a contentious issue, even among health care professionals. Because anorexia has been shown to have biological roots, families, even the most dysfunctional families, are not the sole reason why people become anorexic. Researchers throughout the world say that blaming families for anorexia is much the same as blaming them for diabetes, asthma, or cancer. Also, many anorexics come from close, loving families who are very supportive of them. But some anorexics, including Evelyn Strauss, insist that a stressful family life can play a major role in someone becoming anorexic. Strauss says that while others saw her as a young woman who was happy and successful, inside she was "haunted by feelings of defectiveness and loneliness." Once she stopped eating, anorexia took over and was out of her control. Like most anorexics, Strauss was a perfectionist, yet she never felt like she achieved enough to suit her parents. For instance, once when she brought home a report card that consisted of all A's, her mother criticized her for not getting an A-plus in math. Strauss says that her mother often shouted at her, accusing her of trying to cause trouble by starving herself and losing weight "on purpose." She desperately wanted to get well and feel better, as she explains, "but not the kind of better that gaining weight would bring. I wanted to feel better from the rottenness that had been metastasizing in me before I'd quit eating, the sense that I was invisible except if I was misbehaving or inadequate."[45]

Society and the Media

Some of the hottest debates about anorexia revolve around how much of a role society plays. Even though the disease is far more complex than merely a quest to be thin, many experts still believe that a leading contributor is society's impression that thin equals beautiful—and the media constantly promote this. The "stick-thin" craze began during the 1960s, when Lesley Hornby (better known as Twiggy) rose to international fame as a supermodel. Although Hornby was just naturally thin and not anorexic, her waif-like body became the norm for models, movie stars, and other celebrities. Today, full-color, glossy photos of ultraskinny women such as Kate Moss, Mary-Kate Olsen, and Nicole Ritchie are ubiquitous; and these women are often role models for young girls. At a very early age, girls become aware that fat bodies are undesirable and that women are *supposed to* be thin. They see pictures of thin female stars in movies, in fashion magazines, and on television, and yearn to

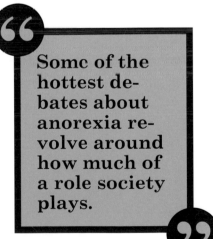

" Some of the hottest debates about anorexia revolve around how much of a role society plays.

look like them. The younger these girls are, the more impressionable they are, and the greater an effect the images have on them. Dr. Ruth Striegel-Moore, who is an eating disorder expert, explains this: "In some ways we all have distorted views of what is beautiful. And the repeated exposure to a particular image teaches you to like that particular image. And we have become so used to seeing extremely thin women that we have learned to think that this is what is beautiful."[46]

A Disease of Mystery

With all the different theories and opinions about what causes anorexia, it is often a controversial topic. Few health care professionals disagree that the disease is highly complex and caused by a combination of factors. Yet much of what has been discovered is theory—no one can say for sure why some people develop anorexia and others do not. As researchers continue studying the disease, they will undoubtedly discover more about it. Hopefully this expanded knowledge will help them learn how to stop anorexia before it starts.

What Causes Anorexia?

66 In my view, biological factors trigger [anorexia] but environmental factors and social pressures make it worse. 99

—Thea Jourdan, "Anorexia Is a Real Disease," *Daily Mail*, September 27, 2005. www.dailymail.co.uk.

Jourdan is a journalist from the United Kingdom who specializes in health-related issues.

66 The reality is that people don't choose [anorexia] and can no more choose to recover from it than you can choose to cure yourself of cancer. 99

—Harriet Brown, "Stigma of Anorexia Keeps Many from Help," *Wisconsin State Journal*, November 10, 2007, p. A8.

Brown is a writer and the mother of a teenage girl who nearly died from anorexia.

* Editor's Note: While the definition of a primary source can be narrowly or broadly defined, for the purposes of Compact Research, a primary source consists of: 1) results of original research presented by an organization or researcher; 2) eyewitness accounts of events, personal experience, or work experience; 3) first-person editorials offering pundits' opinions; 4) government officials presenting political plans and/or policies; 5) representatives of organizations presenting testimony or policy.

66 Anorexia is more than just a problem with food. It's a way of using food or starving oneself to feel more in control of life and to ease tension, anger, and anxiety. 99

—National Women's Health Information Center, "Anorexia Nervosa Frequently Asked Questions," September 2006. www.4woman.gov.

The National Women's Health Information Center is a division of the U.S. Department of Health and Human Services and is devoted to ensuring that women and girls are healthier and have a better sense of well-being.

66 Nothing seemed perfect in my life—like, I didn't get along with my dad and didn't have a lot of friends. I felt like if I could make my *weight* perfect, I'd finally do something right. 99

—Charles Johnson, quoted in Jenni Schaefer, "The Lost Boys," *CosmoGirl*, May 2007, pp. 122–24.

Johnson is a young man from Pennsylvania who struggled with anorexia and bulimia before getting treatment.

66 We need to stop viewing them as a choice. . . . The patients feel guilty, the providers tell them things like they should just eat, parents are blamed, the insurance companies won't fund treatment because they think it's a choice. It's held us back for decades. 99

—Cynthia Bulik, quoted in Tim Whitmire, "Study: Genes May Cause Risk for Anorexia," *USA Today*, April 15, 2007. www.usatoday.com.

Bulik is a psychiatrist at the University of North Carolina at Chapel Hill School of Medicine who specializes in eating disorders.

66 It's not just about women not wanting to eat and wanting to look like a movie star; these are very serious disorders. . . . It was a struggle with relationships, with feelings, with trauma. 99

—Gayle Brooks, quoted in Elizabeth Jensen, "Watching the Battle of Woman vs. Body," *The New York Times*, November 5, 2006. www.nytimes.com.

Brooks is vice president and clinical director for Renfrew Center, an eating disorders clinic in Coconut Creek, Florida.

66 What makes me sad is that people don't understand. An eating disorder is thought of as something you do for vanity. But it's a mental illness. 99

—Brittany Snow, quoted in Lisa Ingrassia, "My Nine-Year Struggle with Anorexia," by Brittany Snow, *People Weekly*, October 15, 2007, p. 89.

Snow, an actress who starred in the movie *Hairspray*, recovered from anorexia after therapy and hospitalization.

66 Fashion is a mirror and many teenagers imitate what they see on the catwalk. 99

—Concha Guerra, quoted in "Madrid Bans Waifs from Catwalk," BBC News, September 13, 2006. http://news.bbc.co.uk.

Guerra is a regional government official in Madrid, Spain.

❝I accepted the cultural message that I read in magazines and saw on television as a child. No one helped me resist the dangerous lie at the heart of this message—'a woman's appearance determines her self-worth'—and I could not resist it on my own.❞

—Julia K. De Pree, *Body Story*. Athens: Ohio University Press, 2004, pp. 2–3.

De Pree, who struggled with anorexia throughout adolescence, is a professor at Agnes Scott College in Atlanta, Georgia.

❝We need to move away from this idea that supermodels are to blame. It is probably not good for them to look as they do. But for anorexics, the desire not to eat and to be thin seems to be already in them and not something they can pick up by looking at a magazine.❞

—Dr. Ian Frampton, quoted in "Models Not Responsible for Anorexia," *Marie Claire*, December 17, 2007. www.marieclaire.co.uk.

Frampton is a psychologist at the University of Exeter in the United Kingdom.

❝Until we discard the victim model and admit that anorexia, though destructive, often fulfills a deep personal need, we can't begin to investigate what makes a person vulnerable to it.❞

—Kate Taylor, "Is Anorexia Genetic?" *Slate*, December 19, 2005. www.slate.com.

Taylor, a recovered anorexic, is the arts reporter at the *New York Sun* and the editor of an anthology of essays about anorexia.

66 Families should not be blamed for causing anorexia. In fact, they are often devastated and suffer from the consequences of this illness. **99**

—Dr. Walter H. Kaye, quoted in "Families Do Not Cause Anorexia Nervosa," University of Pittsburgh Medical Center news release, January 25, 2007. www.medicalnewstoday.com.

Kaye is a psychiatrist and program director of the Eating Disorders Program at the University of California, San Diego.

What Causes Anorexia?

- Anorexics are typically **perfectionists** who have obsessive personalities.

- Many anorexics are **generally unhappy** with their lives and their bodies.

- More than **50 percent** of girls between the ages of 11 and 13 see themselves as overweight.

- Researchers have found that anorexia has **biological roots**, including differences in brain chemistry.

- Studies with twins have shown that more than **50 percent** of someone's chances of developing anorexia is due to genetics.

- Research has shown that males who have **twin sisters** have a markedly higher risk for developing anorexia than other males.

- Environment and society are **contributing factors** toward someone's development of anorexia.

- Nearly **50 percent** of people with anorexia also meet the criteria for depression.

- Young women with **type 1 diabetes** have a higher incidence of eating disorders than young women in the general population.

The Complex Causes of Anorexia

Research has shown that anorexia is a complex disease with numerous contributing and interrelated factors, including biology and genetics, sociocultural influences, and psycho-developmental factors.

Sociocultural Factors

- family dynamioo
- abuse, including sexual abuse
- media exposure
- peer pressure
- lifestyle

Biological Factors

- brain chemistries
- personality structure
- genetics

Psycho-Developmental Factors

- bodily changes during puberty
- life transitions
- sexuality issues

Sources: The Alliance for Eating Disorder Awareness, "Why Do People Get Anorexia?" 2005. www.eatingdisorderinfo.org; Steven Levenkron, *Anatomy of Anorexia*. New York: W.W. Norton & Company, 2000.

The Brain and Distorted Body Image

Why people who suffer from anorexia are unable to see themselves as they really are has puzzled researchers for years. One brain study performed in 2007 by researchers from UCLA resulted in findings that may eventually help scientists solve the mystery. The research focused on a condition known as body dysmorphic disorder (BDD), in which people perceive themselves as ugly and disfigured. Although BDD and anorexia are not the same, both result in sufferers having a seriously distorted body image, and an estimated 30 percent of people with BDD also suffer from eating disorders. Participants included 12 BDD patients and 12 people without the disorder. The researchers used magnetic resonance imaging (MRI) scans to determine how the participants processed visual input when shown digital photos in various stages, from sharp and untouched to blurry. From this, researchers concluded that the BDD patients' brains were hard-wired to see things in a certain way, even if what they "saw" was not really there—meaning that BDD has a biological link and is not attributed solely to environment or society.

MRI scans of the brains of BDD patients showed distinct differences in brain function, with predominant activity on the left side of the brain no matter which visuals they observed.

Source: ScienceDaily, "Distorted Self-Image in Body Image Disorder Due to Visual Brain Glitch, Study Suggests," December 12, 2007. www.sciencedaily.com.

- An August 2005 survey by researchers in the United Kingdom showed that **40 percent** of 5- to 7-year-olds wanted to be thinner than they are.

- Anorexics are **highly sensitive** about failure, frightened of being criticized, and have the desire to always please friends and family.

Body Mass Index

Body mass index (BMI) is a measurement of someone's height in relation to weight and is closely associated with measures of body fat. According to the National Institutes of Health, a healthy BMI ranges from 18.5 to 24.9. A BMI less than 18.5 is considered underweight. The lower the number goes, the more malnourished someone is—and the greater the health risk and chance of death. Anorexics have been known to have dangerously low body mass indexes; Brazilian model Ana Carolina Reston's BMI was just 13.5 at the time of her death at 21 years old in November 2006.

BMI can be calculated by using the following formula:

$$BMI = \frac{(\text{weight in pounds}) \times 703}{\text{height in inches}^2}$$

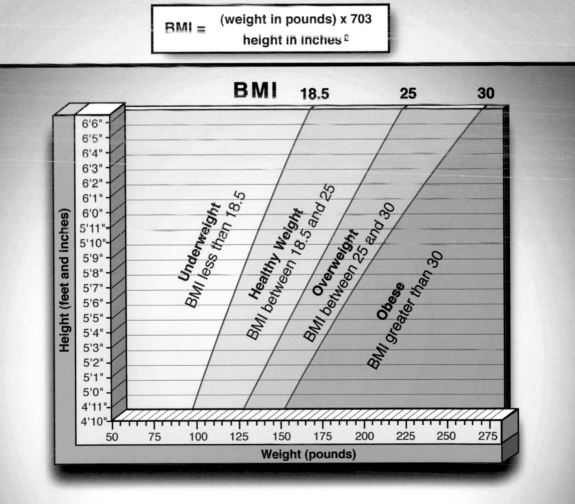

Source: Weight-Control Information Network, "Weight and Waist Management: Tools for Adults," U.S. Department of Health and Human Services, June 2004. http://win.niddk.nih.gov.

- Studies have shown that there is a **greater risk** for developing eating disorders among girls who reach puberty at an early age.

- The average model weighs **23 percent** less than the average woman.

- Canadian surveys have shown that **7.7 percent** of men have a strong fear of being overweight, compared to **18.5 percent** of women.

The Connection Between Anorexia and Emotional Disorders

Health care professionals often find that a large percentage of patients with anorexia also suffer from depression and emotional disorders, and that these disorders are also common in the families of people who have anorexia. It is not known whether emotional disorders can lead to anorexia, increase the likelihood of someone developing it, or if both share a common biologic cause. Following are some of the most common emotional disorders suffered by anorexics.

Emotional Disorder	Characteristics
Obsessive-Compulsive Disorder (OCD): OCD is an anxiety disorder that occurs in nearly 70 percent of patients suffering from anorexia; in fact, some specialists believe that eating disorders could be variants of OCD.	Recurrent or persistent mental images, thoughts, or ideas that result in compulsive behaviors such as repetitive, rigid routines. The compulsive behaviors exhibited by anorexics (obsession with exercise and dieting; weighing every piece of food and counting every calorie; cutting food into tiny pieces; obsession with weight shown on the scale and with mirrors) are signs of OCD.
Phobias	Different types of phobias often precede the onset of anorexia. Among the most common in anorexics are social phobias, in which people are fearful of public humiliation.
Panic Disorder	Periodic attacks of anxiety or terror, known as panic attacks, often begin occurring after the onset of eating disorders.
Post-traumatic Stress Disorder (PTSD)	In one study involving women with serious eating disorders, 74 percent could recall a traumatic event in their lives; more than half showed symptoms of PTSD, an anxiety disorder that occurs in response to (or following) life-threatening circumstances.

Celebrity Anorexics

Since the 1980s, public awareness of anorexia has markedly increased, due in some part to the untimely deaths of famous people who have succumbed to the disease. Following are some of the celebrities who died after losing their battle with anorexia.

Celebrity	Profession	Date of Death	Age at Death	Weight
Karen Carpenter	Pop singer, drummer	Feb. 1983	32	Unknown
Christy Henrich	Gymnast	July 1994	22	60 lbs
Heidi Guenther	Ballerina, Boston Ballet	July 1997	22	93 lbs
Lena Zavaroni	Scottish singer and actress	Oct. 1999	35	70 lbs
Bahne Rabe	German rower and 8-time Olympic gold medalist	Aug. 2001	37	Unknown
Erika Goodman	Ballerina, Joffrey Ballet	Dec. 2004	59	Unknown
Luisel Ramos	Uruguayan fashion model	Aug. 2006	22	98 lbs
Eliana Ramos (sister of Luisel)	Uruguayan fashion model	Feb. 2007	18	Unknown
Ana Carolina Reston	Brazilian fashion model	Nov. 2006	21	88 lbs
Hila Elmalich	Israeli fashion model	Nov. 2007	33	65 lbs

Sources: Martin Beckford, "Sister of Tragic 'Size Zero' Model Found Dead," *Telegraph*, February 15, 2007; Joseph Carman, "Erika Goodman," *Dance Magazine*, May 2005. http://findarticles.com; Stephanie Condron, "Tomato Diet Model Dies of Anorexia," *Telegraph*, November 17, 2006. www.telegraph.co.uk; Simon McGregor-Wood and Karen Mooney, "Did Model Die from Pressure to Be Thin?" ABC News, November 19, 2007; Eric Pace, "Obituary: Christy Henrich, 22, Gymnast Who Suffered from Anorexia," *The New York Times*, July 28, 1994. http://query.nytimes.com; Adena Young, "Battling Anorexia: The Story of Karen Carpenter," *The Quest Behind the Pink Collar*. http://atdpweb.soe.berkeley.edu; "Dying to Be Thin: Share Your Story," PBS NOVA, December 12, 2000. www.pbs.org; "Athletes and Eating Disorders," Eating-Disorder-Information.com. www.eating-disorder-information.com.

What Are the Health Risks of Anorexia?

❝I looked like I had just come back from a concentration camp. My ribs were showing, my cheekbones were coming out, my eyes were sunken in. I had no spirit. I'd lost my soul.❞

—Hannah Sedden, quoted in Peter Overton, "Deadly Seduction."

❝It is difficult to comprehend the complex dynamics that lead to self-inflicted starvation, the vicious cycle begun by limiting food intake to the point that the brain no longer senses hunger, followed by the inexorable damage to the muscles, heart, kidneys and other organs.❞

—Howard Markel, MD, PhD, "Cases: Anorexia Can Strike Boys Too."

People who suffer from anorexia are often easy to spot because the physical symptoms of the disease are obvious. Many anorexics' bodies become so emaciated that they resemble living skeletons. Their skin is deathly pale, their cheeks are sunken in, and there are dark purplish circles under their eyes. Those who knew them in the past may be shocked at their appearance and barely recognize them. Hilde Bruch wrote about her reaction at seeing a 20-year-old anorexic named Alma:

> When she came in for consultation she looked like a walking skeleton, scantily dressed in shorts and a halter, with her legs sticking out like broomsticks, every rib showing,

and her shoulder blades standing up like little wings. . . . Alma's arms and legs were covered with soft hair, her complexion had a yellowish tint, and her dry hair hung down in strings. Most striking was the face—hollow like that of a shriveled-up old woman with a wasting disease, sunken eyes, a sharply pointed nose on which the juncture between bone and cartilage was visible. When she spoke or smiled . . . one could see every movement of the muscles around her mouth and eyes like an animated anatomical representation of the skull.[47]

As horrifying as these symptoms are, they are only what can be seen on the outside; the most severe damages caused by anorexia are the changes taking place inside the body.

Disintegrating Bones

During the 1960s and 1970s, the name Erika Goodman was famous in the world of ballet. Goodman was a ballerina with the esteemed Joffrey Ballet in New York City, and her extraordinary grace and flawless dance techniques captivated audiences whenever she performed. Yet throughout her career she struggled with anorexia, and starved herself to retain her ultrathin dancer's body. It was not uncommon for Goodman to be spotted in a local market

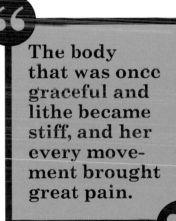

> The body that was once graceful and lithe became stiff, and her every movement brought great pain.

pushing a grocery cart filled with nothing but lettuce. Even today, anorexia is common among ballet dancers because they are under immense pressure to maintain their waif-like bodies. Dr. Linda Hamilton, who danced with the New York City Ballet for 20 years and is now a clinical psychologist, explains how serious this is: "Dancer thin is not like thin on the street. We're talking about 15 percent below your ideal weight for height, which is basically an anorexic weight. If your career is on the line, if the roles are on the line, whether or not you reach that ideal, you will do practically anything."[48]

After battling anorexia for many years, Goodman was stricken with severe osteoporosis when she was in her early 50s. The body that was once graceful and lithe became stiff, and her every movement brought great pain. She discussed this during her appearance on *Dying to Be Thin:* "The really perverse irony of this is that what has been taken away from me are my legs. And for somebody who had always been very flexible, I'm very stiff. And, it's only now that I know. It's only when you're paying for it. You're paying for it then, you see, but you don't know. The cash register hasn't rung. It's ringing now. And it's not until it rings. . . . It's like sleeping. You can have your alarm clock set, but it's not until it goes off that you're going to awaken."[49] At the age of 54 Goodman was so frail that she looked older than her age and could no longer walk without assistance; instead, she slowly shuffled through the streets of New York leaning on a walker for much-needed support. In the fall 2004 she completed her PhD in nutritional science and had hoped to counsel young women who were struggling with eating disorders—but she never got the chance. The following December, Goodman died in her Manhattan apartment at the age of 59.

Such bone diseases are very common among anorexics. The first stage is osteopenia, a loss of bone minerals, which affects almost 90 percent of women with anorexia. This is especially risky for young people because adolescence is a time when enough bone mass is being developed that is supposed to last a lifetime. If bone mass is lost during these critical growth years, the damage is often irreversible. Children, who are typically as tall or taller than their parents, will likely be shorter as adults than they would have been without loss of bone mass. Osteopenia can also lead to dry, brittle bones that fracture easily. Experts say that when adolescent girls and boys develop anorexia, up to two-thirds of them fail to develop strong bones during this vital period of growth. That means a teenager can conceivably have bones that are every bit as fragile as elderly people in their eighties or nineties. Clare Wallmeyer, an anorexic from Australia who has fought the disease for more than 20 years, is now only in her 30s—but she has the bone density of a 100-year-old woman.

About 40 percent of anorexics go on to develop osteoporosis, a more advanced loss of bone mass that ravages the body, as it did Goodman's. The more starved the body becomes the more severe the long-term bone loss, which means the more painful and crippling the permanent damage to the body will be.

A Body Out of Balance

People who starve themselves can do immense damage to vital internal bodily functions. Malnourishment deprives the body of essential vitamins and minerals that are necessary for it to function properly. Electrolytes, for instance, are chemicals such as sodium, calcium, potassium, magnesium, and chloride that are in the bloodstream. A proper balance of electrolytes is essential because they control nerve and muscle impulses, blood sugar levels, kidney and heart functions, and the delivery of oxygen to blood cells. Electrolytes are critical for maintaining a normal heartbeat, and are also primarily responsible for the movement of nutrients into cells and transferring waste out of cells. Any imbalance in electrolytes is extremely dangerous and can lead to serious health consequences, as well as sudden death.

> **Any imbalance in electrolytes is extremely dangerous and can lead to serious health consequences, as well as sudden death.**

Starvation also depletes the store of white blood cells (leukocytes) in the body. This causes a condition known as leucopenia, which affects about 50 percent of anorexic patients. When white blood cells are abnormally low, the immune system loses its ability to fight harmful bacteria, infection, and disease; thus, even a common cold or stomach virus can be deadly. Nearly as common as leucopenia in anorexics is anemia, or a severe deficiency of iron in the bloodstream that reduces red blood cells. A shortage of red blood cells can harm the immune system, as well as inhibit blood from being able to transport adequate amounts of oxygen to the body's organs and tissues; as a result, people with anemia feel tired, weak, and short of breath. An especially serious form of anemia is known as pernicious anemia, in which the body lacks sufficient amounts of vitamin B12 to make enough red blood cells. Pernicious anemia causes blood cells to become too large and not divide normally, which can cause serious damage to the heart and other vital organs, as well as affect the normal working of the nervous system. If not treated, pernicious anemia can lead to a rare but life-threatening disorder called pancytopenia, in which the bone marrow dramatically reduces its production of both red and white blood cells. Pancytopenia also depletes platelets, small blood cells that are necessary for blood clotting. People without sufficient platelets in their blood are in danger of bleeding to death if they are injured.

Anorexia can also cause profound hormonal changes in the body. Starvation lowers the levels of reproductive hormones that are necessary for healthy hearts, bones, and muscle. In women, a deficiency of the estrogen hormone can result in long-term loss of menstruation. Even after treatment and weight gain, an estimated 25 percent of anorexic females never resume menstruating, which can lead to infertility, bone loss, and other serious problems. In males, hormonal abnormalities can result in low levels of testosterone. This can affect bone density, as well as make it difficult for the body to build and maintain muscle. Other hormonal changes include decreased thyroid hormones, which are essential for proper functioning of the thyroid gland, and elevated levels of hormones that regulate stress.

Anorexia's Effect on the Kidneys and Brain

Of all the harm that anorexia can cause to the body, the most potentially lethal damage is how the disease ravages vital organs. For instance, vitamin and mineral deficiencies, electrolyte imbalance, dehydration, and abnormally low blood pressure can lead to irreparable kidney damage and malfunction. When Brazilian model Ana Carolina Reston lost her battle with anorexia in 2006, doctors determined that the cause of death was kidney failure, coupled with severe infection.

> **As the body becomes more malnourished and dehydrated, this starves the brain and causes it to shrink.**

Anorexia also attacks the brain. Brain scan studies have indicated that starvation causes parts of the brain to undergo structural changes and abnormal activity, which can happen in as little as three months after the onset of the disease. As the body becomes more malnourished and dehydrated, this starves the brain and causes it to shrink. Anorexics may suffer from disordered thinking, confusion, insomnia, lack of concentration, blurred vision, numbness in the hands or feet, dizziness and fainting, and in serious cases, seizures. If the anorexia is treated, some of the damage may be reversible; however, permanent damage to the brain is also a distinct possibility, depending on the severity of the disease and the length of time anorexics suffer from it.

"The Heart Was Wasted"

The most life-threatening damage from anorexia is often to the heart, as eating disorder specialists Marcia Herrin and Nancy Matsumoto explain: "As the anorexic body wastes away, so does the heart. Some researchers have noted that even a week or two of severe dieting can lead to substantial loss of heart muscle."[50] This happens because when the body is starving, it must begin digesting organ tissue and muscles for energy—and because the heart is a muscle, the digestion can virtually destroy it. The heart shrinks, growing smaller and weaker and beating at an abnormally slow rate, which markedly increases the risk of heart failure—and this can happen quickly. Heart damage is the most common reason for hospitalization in people with anorexia, and is the leading cause of death. After being starved for so long, the heart can no longer function and simply gives out.

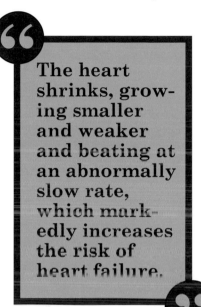

> The heart shrinks, growing smaller and weaker and beating at an abnormally slow rate, which markedly increases the risk of heart failure.

Dr. Howard Markel, a professor of psychiatry at the University of Michigan, diagnosed a 15-year-old boy with anorexia in July 2000. The boy, whose name was Michael, had stopped eating any foods that contained fats because his grandfather had died from a heart attack due to a high-fat diet. Michael became frightened about how fat might harm him and promptly developed a diet for himself that consisted of nothing but water, fat-free turkey, and pita bread. He lost over 45 pounds and suffered from exhaustion, a slow heart rate, dizziness due to low blood pressure, and cold, clammy skin. Markel describes his emaciated appearance: "Only 15, he looks like a wizened old man: the color of his skin gray, his hair falling out and his arm and leg muscles all but melted away." Michael was hospitalized and treated, and gained back a little weight—but after he was discharged he returned to his previous diet and the pounds continued to drop off. Several months later, Markel learned that he had died of a heart attack. "Despite the boy's fears," Markel says, "an autopsy later revealed clean and open arteries, with no cholesterol blockages, but the heart was wasted and shrunken in appearance. I grieved for the loss of a young man no one could reach."[51]

Life After Anorexia

Even if they have recovered, anorexics know that they face a lifelong struggle. Many say that they will never be totally free of the disease, and that is just something they must learn to live with. Although it has been a long time since Marya Hornbacher was caught in the throes of anorexia, she cannot rid herself of the fear that she might someday relapse. She often has bouts of feeling that she is too fat, even though she is underweight for her height. Today, she suffers from lasting effects caused by years of self-starvation—effects that have permanently harmed her body, as she explains:

> The damage to a lot of my systems is irreparable. I can't have kids. My heart is three-fourths the size of a normal heart because the muscle mass was eroded. My bone mass was eroded throughout. I have a heart murmur . . . I'm drastically underweight for my height, although I hide it very well, as many adult women with eating disorders do. If people tell me that I look great, part of the reason is because culturally there's something wrong with their eyes. I look great because I don't look like I'm going to drop dead.[52]

What Are the Health Risks of Anorexia?

" To be in constant pain, to wake up every day and . . . sometimes you can't get out of bed, you're just so tired. "

—Clare Wallmeyer, quoted in Peter Overton, "What a Waste," *60 Minutes*, October 31, 2004, http://sixtyminutes.prev01.ninemsn.com.au.

Wallmeyer is an anorexic from Australia who, along with her twin sister Rachel, has been featured on many national news programs.

" Heart disease is the most common medical cause of death in people with severe anorexia. "

—"Anorexia Nervosa," *The New York Times Health Guide*, reviewed December 13, 2006, by Harvey Simon, MD. http://health.nytimes.com.

Simon is associate professor of medicine at Harvard Medical School and is editor-in-chief of the *New York Times* "Anorexia Nervosa" health article.

* Editor's Note: While the definition of a primary source can be narrowly or broadly defined, for the purposes of Compact Research, a primary source consists of: 1) results of original research presented by an organization or researcher; 2) eyewitness accounts of events, personal experience, or work experience; 3) first-person editorials offering pundits' opinions; 4) government officials presenting political plans and/or policies; 5) representatives of organizations presenting testimony or policy.

66 **She didn't choose anorexia. I know that now, but that doesn't make it any easier to watch her starve herself, and fade away into nothing.** 99

—Jessica Lyons, "Anorexia—the Most Deadly Mental Illness—Is Definitely Not Just About Looking Thin," *Monterey County Weekly*, January 20, 2005. www.montereycountyweekly.com.

Lyons is a staff writer at *Monterey County Weekly* who feared for a friend suffering from anorexia.

66 **[Anorexia and bulimia] are terrifying because they are insidious and stubborn, and they wreak horrible physical damage.** 99

—Diane Guernsey, "Eating Disorders," *Town & Country*, April 2006, pp. 177–81.

Guernsey is a senior editor at *Town & Country* magazine.

66 **Eating disorders linger so long undetected, eroding the body in silence, and then they strike. The secret is out. You're dying.** 99

—Marya Hornbacher, *Wasted: A Memoir of Anorexia and Bulimia*. New York: HarperCollins Publishers, 1998, p. 2.

Hornbacher is an author and journalist who struggled with anorexia and bulimia for most of her life.

❝I couldn't consume a morsel without going to hell and back in my head. I was nearly 19 and at five foot five [165 cm] and six stone [84 pounds], painfully thin. My bones stuck out, my veins stuck out, my hair was falling out and I was always freezing. The doctor diagnosed anorexia nervosa and it stripped me of my future.**❞**

—Grace Bowman, "Making Myself Eat," *Elle Magazine*, April 2006. www.gracebowman.net.

Bowman, a recovered anorexic, is a writer who often does public speaking on eating disorders and young women's issues.

❝Many people with anorexia also have coexisting psychiatric and physical illnesses, including depression, anxiety, obsessive behavior, substance abuse, cardiovascular and neurological complications, and impaired physical development.**❞**

—National Institute of Mental Health, "Eating Disorders," 2007. www.nimh.nih.gov.

The National Institute of Mental Health is the largest scientific organization in the world that is dedicated to mental health research, prevention, and treatment.

❝I was shy, very lost, very skinny, very pale. I looked like I had just come back from a concentration camp. My ribs were showing . . . my eyes were sunken in. I had no spirit. I'd lost my soul.**❞**

—Hannah Sedden, quoted in Peter Overton, "Deadly Seduction," *60 Minutes*, September 18, 2005. http://sixtyminutes.ninemsn.com.au.

Sedden is a young woman who recovered from anorexia through treatment.

> **❝In anorexia nervosa the brain shrinks, a process that may be irreversible.❞**

—Jaet Treasure, RCP: HEalth Implications for Size Zero Culture: Catwalk Models at High Risk of Eating Disorders Have Bad Influence on Public," Royal College of Psychiatry, April 1, 2008. www.politics.co.uk.

Treasure is with Eating Disorders Research Unit, Institute of Psychiatry at Kings, London, UK.

> **❝My body had to eat something in order to survive, so it ate away at my muscle until I had none left. After my muscle, it ate away at whatever it could. I couldn't get up in the morning without every bone in my body aching.❞**

—Kyffin Webb, "Anorexia from Control to Chaos," *Wire Tap Magazine*, February 5, 2002. www.wiretapmag.org.

Webb struggled with anorexia as a teenager and fought to overcome it.

What Are the Health Risks of Anorexia?

- More than **33 percent** of anorexics suffer from anemia, or low red blood cell count.

- An estimated **50 percent** of anorexics suffer from leucopenia, which depletes the body's white blood cells.

- Almost **90 percent** of women with anorexia develop osteopenia, which is loss of bone minerals.

- About **40 percent** of anorexic sufferers develop osteoporosis.

- As many as **95 percent** of hospitalized anorexics have been found to have lower-than-normal heart rates.

- Even after treatment, about **25 percent** of anorexic women never resume menstruating.

- About **10 percent** of anorexic patients have seizures during refeeding.

- An estimated **20 percent** of people suffering from anorexia die from complications related to the disease, including suicide and heart problems.

- In a long-term Danish study of pregnant women with anorexia, **prenatal mortality** was nearly six times greater and incidence of low-birth-weight babies two times greater than expected rates.

Anorexia's Impact on the Body

Self-starvation takes a devastating toll on the entire body and can cause numerous health problems and life-threatening damage.

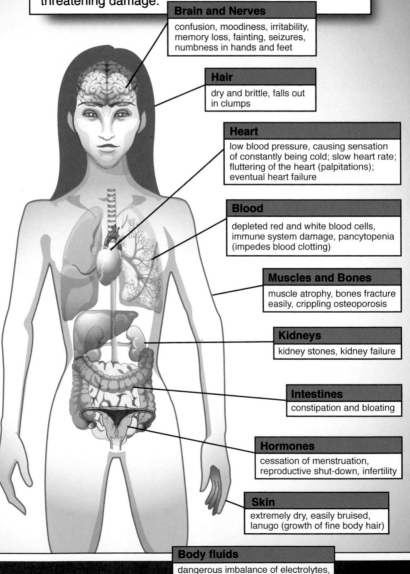

Brain and Nerves
confusion, moodiness, irritability, memory loss, fainting, seizures, numbness in hands and feet

Hair
dry and brittle, falls out in clumps

Heart
low blood pressure, causing sensation of constantly being cold; slow heart rate; fluttering of the heart (palpitations); eventual heart failure

Blood
depleted red and white blood cells, immune system damage, pancytopenia (impedes blood clotting)

Muscles and Bones
muscle atrophy, bones fracture easily, crippling osteoporosis

Kidneys
kidney stones, kidney failure

Intestines
constipation and bloating

Hormones
cessation of menstruation, reproductive shut-down, infertility

Skin
extremely dry, easily bruised, lanugo (growth of fine body hair)

Body fluids
dangerous imbalance of electrolytes, leading to organ damage and death

- Children born to **anorexic mothers** may develop heart disease, kidney and liver malfunctions, and weak bones and teeth.

- A **10 percent** loss of bone mass in the vertebrae can double the risk of vertebral fractures, and a **10 percent** loss of bone mass in the hip can result in a **2.5 times** greater risk of hip fracture.

Anorexia and Osteoporosis

Normal bone and spine   Osteoporotic bone and spine

Starvation can ravage the body's bones, causing a loss of critical bone mass and leading to the painful, crippling disease known as osteoporosis. Osteoporosis commonly affects the spinal column. Normal, healthy bone is hard and strong, with smooth dense tissue making up its honeycomb-like structure. Osteoporosis causes bone structure to become pitted, weakening and aging bones, making them fragile and vulnerable to fractures. Over time, bones continue to weaken and become thinner; eventually bones in the spine can collapse, which causes someone suffering from osteoporosis to become shorter, and to permanently hunch over.

Sources: University of Michigan Health System, "Osteoporosis," July 2005. www.med.umich.edu; WebMD, "Osteoporosis Guide: Picture of Osteoporosis." www.webmd.com.

Anorexia Destroys the Heart

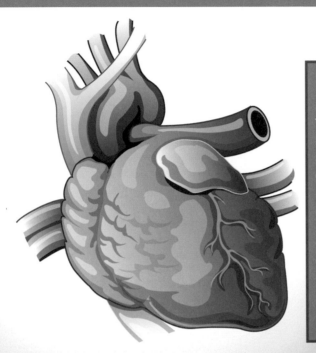

Heart damage is the most common reason for hospitalization in people with anorexia, and is the leading cause of death among anorexics. As the body continues to starve, it satisfies its need for fuel by digesting organ tissue and muscle—and because the heart is a muscle, this can virtually destroy it.

- Dangerous heart rhythms develop including bradycardia, an abnormal slowing of the heart rate from an average 72 beats per minute (BPM) to under 60 BPM

- The heart begins to shrink in size, a condition known as cardiac atrophy, and becomes progressively weaker as starvation continues

- A severe drop in blood pressure due to a condition known as hypotension, which can cause dizziness and fainting, or put the anorexic in a state of shock

- Onset of hypothermia, or a decrease in body temperature to 95 degrees F or lower, causing poor circulation and numbness in the hands and feet, as a well as loss of mental and physical abilities

- Eventually the heart grows so weak that it can no longer function and simply gives out, resulting in cardiac failure and sudden death

Sources: The New York Times, "Anorexia In-Depth Report," December 13, 2006. http://health.nytimes.com; Steven Levenkron, Anatomy of Anorexia. New York: W.W. Norton & Company, 2000.

Can Anorexia Be Cured?

66 This disease changes its victims with every passing day. It makes them sicker. It is rarely 'outgrown.' 99

—Psychotherapist Steven Levenkron, *Anatomy of Anorexia*.

66 Anorexia continues to be difficult to treat. Victims describe an almost spiritual high from starving themselves.... Sadly, we are making little progress against this killer. 99

—Dave Krainacker, MD, PhD, "Anorexia and Karen Carpenter."

While various treatment methods have helped many anorexics recover and go on to live healthy, happy lives, there is no cure for anorexia. It is a complex disease with deep psychological and physiological roots, and treatment must address numerous different factors. One of the biggest challenges facing families of anorexics, as well as health care providers, is that many people with anorexia are not willing to be treated. They may be terrified of gaining weight, or in complete denial of their disease—instead of an illness, they view it as a lifestyle choice that they do not want to give up. Another reason many anorexics reject treatment is that their lives have revolved around anorexia for so long that they fear letting it go. Debra Mittler, who struggled with anorexia for 23 years before recovering, explains this: "Every time I took a step towards healing, something inside me would sabotage it and bring me right back to the anorexia. It was a powerful force that seemed impossible to stop. . . . I was so scared of change that it seemed safer for me to stay the way I was, even if I was going to die."[53]

An "Army of Professionals"

Anorexia treatment programs often involve a team approach, with a number of health care professionals who are experienced at working with eating disorder patients. A team is typically composed of medical doctors, mental health professionals, and nutrition specialists, which Steven Levenkron calls an "army of professionals,"[54] each of whom plays a crucial role in helping anorexics recover.

> While various treatment methods have helped many anorexics recover and go on to live healthy, happy lives, there is no cure for anorexia.

Treatment is broken down into three separate phases: restoring weight, treating psychological problems, and achieving long-term remission or recovery. Many health care experts believe that treatment is most effective if anorexics are hospitalized, although facilities that specialize in eating disorders are rare, and not always accessible to patients and their families. In that case, anorexics may need to seek treatment on an outpatient basis.

The First Steps Toward Recovery

Because malnourishment carries so many serious health risks, the first priority is always restoring the patient to a healthy weight, which is a time known as refeeding. Anorexics receive nutritional counseling during this time to learn the importance of following a healthy diet. If they refuse to eat, or are severely dehydrated, they may be fed through intravenous drips, or tubes (known as nasogastric tubes) that go into the stomach through the nose. The initial refeeding period, even if it is brief, can be risky and dangerous for anorexics. Doctors must monitor their health and vital signs carefully to avoid what is known as refeeding syndrome (RFS), a rare but potentially fatal imbalance in fluids and electrolytes. Weight gain may also cause acute dilation of the stomach, which results in severe abdominal pain, nausea, and vomiting. In the most serious cases, the patient may develop acute pancreatitis; if not treated quickly, it can lead to kidney failure. Another potential side effect of weight gain is edema, or a build-up of fluids in the abdomen or legs. Edema is an early sign that the heart is not yet functioning well enough to handle the increase of fluid that naturally results when anorexics begin to regain weight. This warning must be heeded for the anorexic to survive—if body weight is raised too quickly, the heart, already smaller and weakened because of being severely malnourished, may not be able to manage the sudden increase in blood flow caused by refeeding. This can result in congestive heart failure and death.

Although anorexics are in the refeeding period, it is not uncommon for them to lose weight, or gain and lose the same pound over and over, even if they are on a high-calorie diet. As their body temperatures rise to a normal level, their metabolism responds by racing, which causes them to burn off calories. Walter Kaye says that is one reason why so many anorexics relapse, as he explains: "It's hard to gain enough weight to truly recover, and even harder to maintain it."[55]

Along with medical treatment, anorexics participate in intense psychotherapy sessions, either individually or in groups. Therapy helps them address the psychological reasons for the illness, such as obsessive behaviors, distorted body image, destructive thoughts, family dysfunction, or interpersonal conflict. Also, gaining weight can be a frightening experience for anorexics who are, by nature, terrified of getting fat. According to eating disorder specialist Carolyn Hodges, this can inhibit the anorexic's recovery. She adds that such obsessive thoughts increase as anorexics continue to be re-fed, and the irrational fears of gaining weight often last for several months or longer.

Treatment Challenges

Most anorexia treatment programs do not involve the anorexic's family, which can be stressful for parents as Peg Tyre explains: "Too often these days, parents aren't so much banished from the treatment process as sidelined, watching powerlessly as doctors take what can be extreme measures to make their children well."[56] Such programs can be especially frightening for young children, who may be terrified at the notion of being away from home for longer periods of time. Another challenge is that lengthy stays in hospitals and treatment centers are so expensive that many people simply cannot afford to pay for them. The typical cost for inpatient treatment ranges from $500 to $2,000 per day, with the average cost for a month of hospitalization about $30,000, and these costs are often not covered by health insurance. Even outpatient care can be expensive, costing as much as $100,000 per year. As a result, only about 1 out of 10 people who suffer from anorexia get treated for it.

> "Anorexics may receive the finest treatment available, but anorexia is still tough to beat."

Anorexics may receive the finest treatment available, but anorexia is still tough to beat. The only way they can fully recover is by slaying the demons that have long controlled them and overcoming their distorted view of reality, and that can be a daunting task. The Mayo Clinic explains: "Even for people who do want to get better, the pull of anorexia can be difficult to overcome. For some, anorexia is a lifelong battle. Even if symptoms subside, people with anorexia remain vulnerable and may have a relapse during periods of high stress or during triggering situations."[57]

Family-Centered Treatment

A treatment program known as the Maudsley Approach was developed in the early 1980s at the Maudsley Hospital in London. Daniel le Grange began training at the hospital in 1986 and developed a passion for the treatment method, especially in its application to adolescents with anorexia. In 1994, when le Grange returned to the United States, he introduced the program to his colleagues at Stanford University. The major difference between the Maudsley Approach and other methods is that Maudsley is family-based treatment (FBT)—parents play an integral role in their child's recovery. Also, the program requires no inpatient hospitalization; rather, patients participate in intensive outpatient treatment in which the entire family is involved. Le Grange is convinced that parents should play a major role in their child's recovery, as he explains: "We empower parents to do the job that they normally do well, which is to take care of their kids."[58]

The Maudsley Approach starts with a team of doctors, therapists, and nutritionists, meeting with parents and the anorexic child to explain that anorexia is just as serious and life-threatening as diseases such as cancer or diabetes. The team makes it clear that for the anorexic, food is medicine. Parents receive nutritional counseling, including a strict regimen of calories, carbohydrates, and fiber that the anorexic must eat every day. The parents and other family members also learn how to provide the anorexic with necessary support. After participating in a few practice meals in a hospital or doctor's office, they are sent home to have a meal together. This family mealtime is a core component of the Maudsley Approach; parents must be present for all the anorexic child's meals and supervise his or her eating closely. They continuously reinforce that food is medicine and must be eaten; refusing to eat is simply not an option. Even if mealtimes stretch over several hours, the child is still expected to clean up every bite.

The success rate for the Maudsley Approach has been phenomenally high. One study conducted in 1997 showed that 90 percent of anorexics who participated in Maudsley programs had recovered or made significant progress, and a second study in 2002 found that 90 percent of the patients had fully recovered. Other studies have resulted in the same high success rate.

A Story of Recovery

Harriet Brown's daughter, Kitty, was diagnosed with anorexia when she was 14 years old. For no apparent reason Kitty just stopped eating, began exercising for hours every night, and constantly obsessed over food and meals. At 4 feet 11 inches (150 cm) tall and just 71 pounds (32.2 kg), Kitty was wasting away and Brown was desperate to help her. The girl's body was so emaciated that each angle and curve of her bones was clearly visible under her skin—yet she could not see this, and continued to insist that she was fat. After trying several different treatment methods and seeing no progress, Brown decided to try the Maudsley Approach. "We didn't know if Maudsley would work," she says. "We didn't know if it was, objectively speaking, the best choice. But anything was better than watching Kitty disappear, ounce by ounce, obscured by the creature who spoke with her voice and looked out through her eyes. Anything."[59]

> " **The success rate for the Maudsley Approach has been phenomenally high.** "

After consulting with le Grange, Brown and her husband lined up their own treatment team, which included a pediatrician, a psychiatrist, a therapist, and a nutritionist. They supervised all of Kitty's meals and insisted that she eat them, telling her that they did not care how long it took. One night Brown sat on Kitty's bed for 2 hours until the girl finished drinking a milkshake. On another occasion Kitty spent 45 minutes eating a small piece of cake; afterward, she lay her head on the table and sobbed over how scary the experience had been. "At age 4, Kitty went for a pony ride and was seated on an enormous quarter horse," says Brown. "When the horse reared, she just held on. Afterward I asked if she'd been scared. 'Not really,' she said. 'Can I go again?' This was the child who was now terrified by a slice of chocolate cake."[60]

Kitty's recovery period was excruciating for her parents. She lived in constant terror of gaining weight, sometimes refused to eat, and often lashed out angrily during meals, accusing her parents of trying to make her fat. Yet she slowly began to make progress, and about a year after her treatment started, she had reached her target weight and was doing well both psychologically and socially. As optimistic as Brown is today, however, she still fears for her daughter, as is common with parents who have lived through anorexia with a child. "The demon is part of our family now, lurking in the shadows," she says. "We will never forget it. . . . Is Kitty cured? Will she ever be cured? There are so many questions I can't answer."[61]

The Mandometer Method

Some eating disorder specialists have a different theory about anorexia. Those who ascribe to the Mandometer method do not agree with the experts who say that anorexia is a mental health disorder. Instead, they claim that starvation comes first; as anorexics gain pleasure from dieting and losing weight, they starve themselves even more and the result is psychological symptoms such as obsessive-compulsive disorder and depression. One researcher who shares that belief is Dr. Cecelia Bergh, who explains: "Everyone has it backward. The disordered eating causes the psychological problems, not the other way around."[62] Bergh advocates Mandometer treatment, which originated at the Karolinska Institute in Sweden in 1992 and was later expanded to clinics in Amsterdam and Australia. In September 2004, the first Mandometer facility, the Mandometer Clinic, opened in the United States in San Diego, California.

Mandometer treatment revolves around the basic concept that anorexics do not know how to eat properly, and they must relearn it by retraining their appetite and listening to it. Advocates of the treatment say that once patients are taught how to eat again, the mental symptoms eventually disappear. The program uses a unique three-pronged approach to healing: biofeedback, heat therapy, and social support. At the California clinic, treatment usually lasts for 12 months and begins with the anorexic being evaluated by a medical doctor. If necessary, patients may be hospitalized first and treated under the direction of the clinic's medical director. Then they are evaluated by a multidisciplinary team of professionals and assigned a personal case manager, all of whom have been trained in Mandometer treatment.

At the heart of the program is the Mandometer, a computerized disk-like biofeedback device that is customized for each patient and is connected to a scale. The high-tech gadget is designed to help patients relearn normal eating and to reconnect with natural feelings of hunger and fullness. Patients spend their days at the clinic, and at night they

> **Because Mandometer therapists do not believe that anorexia is a mental illness, traditional psychotherapy is not part of the program, nor are patients given antidepressants or other drugs.**

stay in nearby apartments. They attend meals in a lunchroom and fill their own plates with food. At tables, they put their plates on the Mandometer and the screen tells them if they have gotten the right amount of food. As they eat, curves on the screen indicate how much they have eaten, whether they are eating at the proper rate (anorexics typically eat far too slowly), and how full they should be feeling.

After meals, patients participate in heat therapy, either lying down for an hour in a small room heated to 112 degrees F (44.4 degrees C), or wearing specially designed jackets with built-in heating devices. According to Bergh, this is a crucial step after meals, as she explains: "The heat keeps them calm and helps prevent the anxiety that typically hits after they eat, making them want to purge or exercise."[63] After the heat treatment, patients stay at the clinic until after dinner, and then return to their apartments. At some point during the day or evening they meet with their case managers to talk about whatever they are feeling. The frequency of these sessions depends on how long the anorexic has been in treatment; at first, patients meet with their case manager five times per week, gradually reducing the sessions to one per week, and finally to once every other week. Because the Mandometer philosophy is that anorexia is not a mental illness, traditional psychotherapy is not part of the program, nor are patients given antidepressants or other drugs.

The Mandometer clinics reportedly have a 75 percent success rate. The clinic's relapse rate is also impressive; depending on a number of factors, the typical relapse rate for anorexics is as high as 50 percent within a year after treatment, whereas Mandometer's relapse rate is just 10 percent within 5 years after treatment.

What Tomorrow Holds

As awareness of anorexia continues to grow, and research reveals more about what causes it, health care professionals are becoming more optimistic about helping people who struggle with anorexia. Yet they are cautiously optimistic because it is still a deadly disease that afflicts millions of people of all ages and all walks of life. No one can say whether it will ever be completely eliminated, or even reduced. But those who have recovered often feel like they have been given a new chance at life. One of the survivors is Laura Penny, a young woman from the United Kingdom who considers herself one of the lucky ones. She shares her thoughts:

> From the withered, starved, lonely little world in which I lived before going into the hospital, with only my books and stories for company, I'm becoming human again—perhaps for the first time—and discovering a whole new world of which I've had no previous experience, and it's all hopelessly exciting. . . . Having starved myself of life for so long, I'm now ravenous for it.[64]

Can Anorexia Be Cured?

" Anorexia is often an ongoing, lifelong battle. "

—Mayo Clinic Staff, "Anorexia Nervosa: Treatment," December 20, 2007.

The Mayo Clinic is a world-renown medical facility that is dedicated to the diagnosis and treatment of virtually every type of illness.

" As I fight to take life back into my own hands, I realize I am going to have to do something very scary. I'm going to have to let go of my best friend, Anorexia. She . . . was never very good at being a best friend, anyway. "

—Kyffin Webb, "Anorexia from Control to Chaos," *WireTap Magazine*, February 5, 2002. www.wiretapmag.org.

Webb struggled with anorexia as a teenager and fought to overcome it.

* Editor's Note: While the definition of a primary source can be narrowly or broadly defined, for the purposes of Compact Research, a primary source consists of: 1) results of original research presented by an organization or researcher; 2) eyewitness accounts of events, personal experience, or work experience; 3) first-person editorials offering pundits' opinions; 4) government officials presenting political plans and/or policies; 5) representatives of organizations presenting testimony or policy.

❝People say, 'Once an anorexic, always an anorexic.' We don't believe that. We feel people can recover.❞

—Cecilia Bergh, PhD, quoted in Ginny Graves, "No Time to Lose," *Self,* June 2006, pp. 98–100.

Bergh is an eating disorder researcher who helped develop the Mandometer treatment program.

❝As many as 10 to 20 percent of people diagnosed with anorexia nervosa die of it and its complications, which include fluid and electrolyte abnormalities, heart failure, and suicide.❞

"Struggling with Eating Disorders," *Your Health Now,* Merck, vol. 2, issue 1, 2006. www.merck.com.

Merck is one of the world's largest pharmaceutical companies.

❝Faced with a girl who has decided to let herself die there's nothing you can really do.❞

—Massimo Cuzzolaro, quoted in Web Editor, "Anorexia Alarm for Italian Mums," *Italy,* April 7, 2007.

Cuzzolaro is professor of psychiatry at La Sapienza University in Rome.

66 Anorexics are often told to stop dieting, to listen to their body and to give it what it wants. But the reality is that they are listening to their bodies, and their bodies are telling them not to eat. The truth is, they have to stop listening. 99

—Dr. Shan Guisinger, quoted in Ellen Ruppel Shell, "The Ancestry of Anorexia,"
The Boston Globe, December 30, 2003. www.boston.com.

Guisinger is a psychologist from Missoula, Montana, who specializes in eating disorders.

---

66 With comprehensive treatment, most teenagers can be relieved of the symptoms or helped to control eating disorders. 99

—American Academy of Child & Adolescent Psychiatry (AACAP), "Teenagers
with Eating Disorders," July 2004. www.aacap.org.

AACAP is a professional association that is dedicated to treating and improving the quality of life for young people suffering from mental, behavioral, or developmental disorders, including anorexia and bulimia.

---

66 [Anorexia is] something that will make you feel more miserable than you've ever felt in your entire life and yet it's enticing and you can't let go of it because it's the only thing you have. 99

—Lizzy Eastman, quoted in Peter Overton, "Deadly Seduction," *60 Minutes*,
September 18, 2005. http://sixtyminutes.ninemsn.com.au.

Eastman is a young woman from San Francisco who suffers from anorexia, and who has been criticized for her "pro-anorexia" Web site.

❝Your search for happiness on the scale is nothing more than looking for gold at the end of a rainbow. It isn't there and it never will be no matter how low the numbers fall.❞

—Alliance for Eating Disorder Awareness, "Eating Disorders," October 2003. www.eatingdisorderinfo.org.

Alliance for Eating Disorder Awareness is an organization that strives to educate young people about the dangers of eating disorders while stressing the importance of a positive body image and healthy self-esteem.

❝The depth of self hatred and hopelessness that people feel when they experience anorexia nervosa often leads them and their families to feel that there is no escape from the illness.❞

—Chris Thornton, quoted in Graeme Cole, "Silverchair Singer Not Alone in Struggle Against Anorexia," Wesley Mission press release, June 8, 2004. www.wesleymission.org.au.

Thornton is a clinical psychologist from Australia who specializes in treatment of eating disorders.

❝New research findings are showing that some of the 'traits' in individuals who develop anorexia nervosa are actual 'risk factors' that might be treated early on.❞

—"About Mental Illness: Anorexia Nervosa," National Alliance on Mental Illness, reviewed by Barbara Wolfe, RN, PhD, June 2003. www.nami.org.

Wolfe is with Harvard Medical School's department of psychiatry.

Can Anorexia Be Cured?

- There is **no cure** for anorexia.

- Only **10 percent** of people with eating disorders receive treatment.

- Treatment for anorexia is extremely expensive—ranging from $500 to $2,000 per day, with the average cost for a month of hospitalization about **$30,000.**

- Outpatient anorexia treatment can cost up to **$100,000 per year**.

- Studies have shown that **5 to 10 percent** of anorexics die within 10 years after developing the disease; **18 to 20 percent** will be dead after 20 years; and only **30 to 40 percent** ever fully recover.

- The average relapse rate for anorexics is **40 to 50 percent**.

- Studies have shown that up to **90 percent** of anorexics who participate in Maudsley programs either fully recover or make significant progress.

- The Mandometer Clinic in San Diego, California, reports a **75 percent** success rate and only a **10 percent** relapse rate.

- Typical anorexia treatment programs last from **10 to 12 weeks**.

- Initial weight gain during anorexia treatment is limited to **1 to 2 pounds** a week.

Anorexia Treatment

Although treatment programs vary widely from facility to facility, most eating disorder specialists recommend a team approach that includes medical doctors, mental health professionals, and nutrition specialists, each of whom plays a crucial role in helping anorexics recover. The effectiveness of any treatment program depends on numerous factors including the individual situation, attitude of the person involved (willingness to be treated versus hostility or denial), and the severity of the disease. The following illustrates what is typically included in an anorexic's treatment.

Phase 1   Weight restoration (refeeding)

- Physical exam: Vital signs are checked; tests for possible electrolyte imbalances and protein levels; determine any liver, kidney, and thyroid damage; bone density tests to determine loss of bone mass; electrocardiogram to check for heart damage

- Refeeding begins; if patient is too sick to eat, or refuses to eat, initial refeeding may be accomplished with intravenous drips or nasogastric tubes

- Patient receives nutritional counseling to learn about essential vitamins and minerals, and the importance of a healthy diet

- Patient is carefully monitored throughout early refeeding to avoid a deadly disorder known as refeeding syndrome

- Eventually work up to three meals a day and increase in calories

Phase 2   Psychological counseling

- Psychotherapy sessions, either private or in a group, help patient sort out psychological reasons contributing toward anorexia, destructive thoughts, family dysfunction, and interpersonal conflicts

- As patient gains weight, therapy addresses obsessive thoughts and fear of becoming fat, as well as realistic versus distorted view of body image

- Antidepressants may be prescribed to help with depression and fears

Phase 3   Achieving long-term remission or recovery

- Keep the patient's weight stabilized, ensure healthy BMI

- Therapy continues; goal in this phase is to reduce or eliminate behaviors or thoughts that contribute toward anorexia, and to prevent relapse

- Patient is encouraged to be frank about feelings and attitudes, and to report any relapses without fear of reprisal

Sources: National Association for Anorexia Nervosa and Associated Eating Disorders (ANAD), "Facts About Eating Disorders." www.anad.org; The New York Times, "Anorexia In-Depth Report," December 13, 2006. http://health.nytimes.com; Mayo Clinic,

- Since 1987, hospitalizations for eating disorders in Canada have increased by 34 percent among young women under the age of 15 and by **29 percent** among 15 to 24 year olds.

- A study by researchers at the University of Virginia showed that anorexics who attempt suicide use **highly lethal methods**, which indicates a strong wish to die.

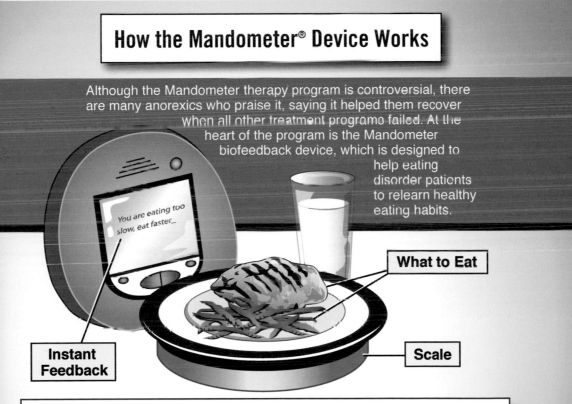

How the Mandometer® Device Works

Although the Mandometer therapy program is controversial, there are many anorexics who praise it, saying it helped them recover when all other treatment programs failed. At the heart of the program is the Mandometer biofeedback device, which is designed to help eating disorder patients to relearn healthy eating habits.

You are eating too slow, eat faster_

What to Eat

Instant Feedback

Scale

- Scale is hooked up to the computer
- Empty plate is placed on the scale, and adjusted for the plate's weight
- Food is slowly placed on the plate until the agreed-upon quantity is reached
- Patient begins eating when prompted
- Throughout the meal, a graph on the screen records progress; feedback is offered, such as "You are eating too slow, eat faster" or "You are eating too fast, slow down"
- Also throughout the meal, the patient records rate of fullness (satiety); computer compares this to normal ranges
- After the meal, the patient is told his or her progress

Sources: "The Mandometer®—a Breakthrough Eating Disorder Treatment Technology That Defeats Anorexia and Bulimia," Mandometer®. www.wscreative.com; Ginny Graves, "No Time to Lose," *Self*, June 2006, p.99.

Anorexia: A Lasting Disease

Anorexia is a disease with grim statistics; research has shown that only 30 to 40 percent of anorexics ever fully recover, and even that cannot be known for sure. Because so many anorexics do not get treatment, there is no way for health care professionals to know the exact number of patients who recover from the disease, die from its effects, or commit suicide. The following chart shows the average length of time that people typically battle anorexia.

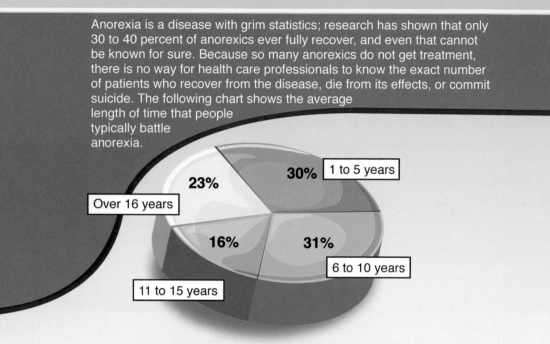

Source: National Association for Anorexia Nervosa and Associated Eating Disorders (ANAD), "Facts About Eating Disorders." www.anad.org.

- There is no evidence to show that antidepressants or other medications are effective in the critical first phase of restoring anorexics to a healthy weight.

- Studies have shown that European countries have an overall success rate of between **30 and 40 percent** for anorexia and bulimia.

Key People and Advocacy Groups

Academy for Eating Disorders (AED): Founded in 1993 by a group of clinicians and researchers, the AED provides education and training for mental health professionals, as well as promotes research, treatment, and prevention for eating disorders.

Alliance for Eating Disorders Awareness: The Alliance for Eating Disorders Awareness educates young people about eating disorders, while providing a wealth of educational information to parents and health care providers about the warning signs, dangers, and risks of anorexia, bulimia, and related illnesses.

Anorexia Nervosa and Related Eating Disorders, Inc. (ANRED): ANRED increases public awareness and understanding of the health risks of anorexia, bulimia, and other eating disorders by providing educational and research materials.

Cecelia Bergh, PhD: Bergh is a Swedish scientist and the chief executive of AB Mondo, as well as the founder of the Mandometer Clinic in California. She was also part of the development team that created the Mandometer biofeedback device.

Hilde Bruch: In 1978, Bruch, a psychoanalyst, wrote *The Golden Cage: The Enigma of Anorexia Nervosa*, one of the first books ever written about the disease.

Cynthia Bulik: A renowned eating disorders specialist and researcher, Bulik is a psychiatrist and professor at the University of North Carolina at Chapel Hill School of Medicine.

Eating Disorders Coalition (EDC): It is EDC's goal to advance the recognition of eating disorders as a national health priority by promoting awareness among the public and policy makers; supporting initiatives on behalf of healthy development of children; and increasing resources for research, education, prevention, and improved training.

Karolinska Institute: Located in Stockholm, Sweden, the Karolinska Institute is one of Europe's largest medical universities and is also Sweden's largest center for medical training and research. In 1992, the world's first Mandometer clinic was founded at the Institute.

Walter H. Kaye, MD: A renowned researcher and eating disorders specialist, Kaye is a psychiatrist and program director of the Eating Disorders Program at the University of California, San Diego.

Daniel le Grange, PhD: Le Grange is associate professor of psychiatry at the University of Chicago, as well as director of the school's Eating Disorders Program. During his five years at the Maudsley Hospital in London, le Grange helped create the Maudsley Approach for eating disorder therapy. Later, he introduced the program in the United States and wrote Maudsley treatment manuals for physicians and therapists, as well as a book for parents.

Steven Levenkron, MS: A well-known New York City psychotherapist, Levenkron specializes in eating disorders and has written a number of books on anorexia, bulimia, and cutting.

Maudsley Hospital: Located in South London, Maudsley Hospital was where the Maudsley Approach to eating disorders was first developed. Today, the hospital's Eating Disorder Service provides Maudsley family-based therapy to people who are suffering from anorexia or bulimia.

National Association of Anorexia Nervosa and Associated Disorders (ANAD): Launched in 1976, ANAD is the oldest eating disorder organization in the United States. It seeks to increase awareness of eating disorders by educating the public and health care professionals, and serves as a resource center that provides information about eating disorders, including sources and facilities for treatment.

National Eating Disorders Association (NEDA): NEDA's goal is to expand public understanding and prevention of eating disorders, while promoting access to quality treatment and support for families through education, advocacy, and research.

David Rosen, MD, MPH: Rosen is a well-known eating disorder specialist and professor at the University of Michigan Medical School.

Clare and Rachel Wallmeyer: Perhaps the most famous anorexics in the world, the Wallmeyers are identical twins from Melbourne, Australia, who have suffered from anorexia for more than 20 years, and have been featured on many national news programs in an effort to increase awareness of the dangers of anorexia.

Chronology

1873

In an address to the British Medical Association, Queen Victoria's chief physician, William Wythe Gull, coins the term *anorexia nervosa,* meaning "nervous loss of appetite," to describe young girls who starve themselves to maintain tiny waistlines.

1978

Psychiatrist Hilde Bruch, MD, publishes one of the first books about anorexia called *The Golden Cage: The Enigma of Anorexia Nervosa.*

1994

Dr. Daniel le Grange introduces the Maudsley Approach to eating disorder therapy in the United States.

1976

National Association of Anorexia Nervosa and Associated Disorders (ANAD) is founded, and becomes the first organization in the United States devoted to eating disorders.

1983

Popular singer and drummer Karen Carpenter dies of cardiac arrest as a complication of anorexia, thus increasing public awareness of the dangers of the disease.

1900   **1960**   **1970**   **1980**   **1990**

1966

Lesley Hornby, better known as "Twiggy," rises to international fame as a supermodel, and skinny bodies become the norm in the world of fashion.

1980

Anorexia nervosa is officially classified as a psychiatric illness in the third edition of the *Diagnostic and Statistical Manual of Mental Disorders* (DSM).

1985

Renfrew Center, America's first residential facility for women with eating disorders, opens in Philadelphia.

Early 1980s

The Maudsley Approach to eating disorder therapy, also known as family based treatment (FBT), is developed at the Maudsley Hospital in London.

1992

Mandometer therapy is developed at the Karolinska Institute in Sweden.

2000

Based on studies with twins, researchers at Virginia Commonwealth University conclude that more than 50 percent of the risk for developing anorexia could be due to genetics.

2006

Based on studies with twins, researchers at the University of North Carolina at Chapel Hill and Sweden's Karolinska Institute conclude that 56 percent of the risk for developing anorexia is attributable to genetics.

Uruguayan fashion model Luisel Ramos dies of heart failure at age 22 from complications of anorexia.

Brazilian fashion model Ana Carolina Reston, age 21, dies of kidney failure and infection caused by anorexia.

In the first ban of its kind, the Spanish Association of Fashion Designers bans models with a body mass index of less than 18 from participating in the prestigious Fashion Week show in Madrid.

| 2000 | 2002 | 2004 | 2006 | 2008 |

2004

The Mandometer Clinic opens in San Diego, California, the first U.S. eating disorder facility to use the Mandometer method of treatment for eating disorders.

1999

A billboard featuring a full-color photograph of the three female stars of the hit television show *Friends* appears in Sioux Falls, South Dakota, with copy that reads "Cute anorexic chicks." The billboard is removed because of protests by eating disorder organizations.

Through brain studies with recovered anorexics, Dr. Walter Kaye discovers abnormally high levels of serotonin, an indication of differences in anorexics' brain chemistry.

2007

The National Institute of Mental Health (NIMH) funds a groundbreaking four-year research project to study the role of genetics in the development of anorexia. The study is a collaborative effort, involving six American and three international research institutions.

Fashion model Eliana Ramos (sister of Luisel) dies at the age of 18 from complications of anorexia.

Photographer Oliviero Toscani shocks Europe with his anti-anorexia advertising campaign, including billboards and newspaper ads that feature the anorexic, emaciated French actress Isabelle Caro posing in the nude. The billboards, with the copy "No Anorexia," appear during Fashion Week in Milan.

Israeli fashion model Hila Elmalich dies at the age of 33 of heart failure caused by anorexia.

Related Organizations

Academy for Eating Disorders (AED)
111 Deer Lake Road, Suite 100
Deerfield, IL 60015
phone: (847) 498-4274
fax: (847) 480-9282
e-mail: info@aedweb.org
Web site: www.aedweb.org

AED is a professional organization that provides education and training for mental health professionals, and also promotes excellence in research, treatment, and prevention of eating disorders. A variety of research papers, abstracts, and news releases can be downloaded from the Web site.

Alliance for Eating Disorders Awareness
PO Box 13155
North Palm Beach, FL 33408-3155
phone: (866) 662-1235
fax: (561) 841-0972
e-mail: info@eatngdisorderinfo.org
Web site: www.eatingdisorderinfo.org

This organization strives to educate young people about the dangers of eating disorders, while stressing the importance of self-esteem and a positive body image. Numerous materials related to anorexia are available on the Web site, including statistics, causes, success stories, risk factors, and getting help.

American Academy of Child and Adolescent Psychiatry (AACAP)
3615 Wisconsin Avenue NW
Washington, DC 20016-3007
phone: (202) 966-7300
fax: (202) 966-2891

e-mail: info@aacap.org

Web site: www.aacap.org

AACAP is a professional medical association that is dedicated to treating and improving the quality of life for young people suffering from mental, behavioral, or developmental disorders and their families. A number of anorexia research papers are available on the Web site, and there is also a special "Resources for Families" section that has a variety of information.

American Dietetic Association (ADA)

120 South Riverside Plaza, Suite 2000

Chicago, IL 60606-6995

phone: (800) 877-1600

fax: (312) 899-4812

e-mail: info@eatright.org

Web Site: www.eatright.org

The ADA is America's largest organization of food and nutrition professionals, with about 75 percent of its members being registered dieticians. A wealth of nutrition-related research can be found on the Web site, including articles relating specifically to anorexia and other eating disorders.

American Psychiatric Association (APA)

1000 Wilson Boulevard, Suite 1825

Arlington, VA 22209-3901

phone: (703) 907-7300

fax: (703) 907-1082

e-mail: apa@psych.org

Web site: www.psych.org

The APA works to ensure the humane care and effective treatment for people with mental disorders. Numerous publications and journals such as the *American Journal of Psychiatry* and *Psychiatric News* are available on the Web site.

Anorexia Nervosa and Related Eating Disorders, Inc. (ANRED)

PO Box 5102

Eugene, OR 97405

phone: (503) 344-1144

e-mail: jarinor@rio.com

Web site: www.anred.com

ANRED's goal is to educate the public about the health risks of anorexia, bulimia, and other eating disorders. The Web site includes self-help tips and information about recovery and prevention.

Eating Disorders Coalition (EDC)

611 Pennsylvania Avenue SE #423

Washington, DC 20003-4303

phone: (202) 543-9570

e-mail: manager@eatingdisorderscoalition.org

Web site: www.eatingdisorderscoalition.org

EDC seeks to advance the recognition of eating disorders as a public health priority. Material available on the Web site includes fact sheets, information about health insurance coverage, legislative updates, and statistics.

National Association of Anorexia Nervosa and Associated Disorders (ANAD)

P.O. Box 7

Highland Park, IL 60035

phone: (847) 433-3996

fax: (847) 433-4632

e-mail: info@anad.org

Web site: www.anad.org

ANAD educates the public and health care professionals to be more aware of eating disorders and methods of treatment, and acts as a resource center that provides information about eating disorders, including sources and facilities for treatment. The Web site includes "News of Interest," links to eating disorder clinics, statistics, and warning signs/symptoms of anorexia and bulimia.

National Eating Disorders Association (NEDA)

603 Stewart Street, Suite 803

Seattle, WA 98101

phone: (206) 382-3587

fax: (206) 829-8501

e-mail: info@nationaleatingdisorders.org

Web site: www.nationaleatingdisorders.org

NEDA is dedicated to expanding public understanding and prevention of eating disorders and promoting access to quality treatment for those affected along with support for their families through education, advocacy, and research. The Web site offers position statements, news releases, resources for anorexia sufferers and families, and research papers.

National Institute of Mental Health (NIMH)

Science Writing, Press, and Dissemination Branch

6001 Executive Boulevard, Room 8184, MSC 9663

Bethesda, MD 20892-9663

phone: (866) 615-6464

fax: (301) 443-4279

e-mail: nimhinfo@nih.gov

Web site: www.nimh.nih.gov

NIMH seeks to reduce mental illness and behavioral disorders through research, and supports science that will profoundly affect the diagnosis, treatment, and prevention of mental disorders. The Web site provides many different research publications on anorexia, as well as statistics and current news.

For Further Research

Books

Joan Jacobs Brumberg, *Fasting Girls: The History of Anorexia Nervosa.* New York: Vintage Books, 2000.

Sheryle Cruse, *Thin Enough: My Spiritual Journey Through the Living Death of an Eating Disorder.* Birmingham, AL: New Hope, 2006.

Julia K. De Pree, *Body Story.* Athens: Ohio University Press, 2004.

Lori Gottlieb, *Stick Figure: A Diary of My Former Self.* New York: Simon & Schuster, 2000.

Gary A. Grahl, *Skinny Boy: A Young Man's Battle and Triumph over Anorexia.* Clearfield, UT: American Legacy Media, 2007.

Lauren Greenfield, *Thin.* San Francisco: Chronicle Books, 2006.

Daniel A. Leone (ed.), *Anorexia.* San Diego, CA: Greenhaven Press, 2001.

Steven Levenkron, *Anatomy of Anorexia.* New York/London: W.W. Norton & Company, 2000.

Aimee Liu, *Gaining: The Truth About Life After Eating Disorders.* New York: Warner Books, 2007.

Morgan Menzie, *Diary of an Anorexic Girl.* Nashville, TN: W Publishing Group, 2003.

Katie Metcalf, *Anorexia: A Stranger in the Family.* Pembroke Dock, Wales: Accent Press, 2007.

Anna Paterson, *Fit to Die: Men and Eating Disorders.* London, UK: Paul Chapman Educational Publishing, 2004.

Christie Pettit, *Empty: A Story of Anorexia.* Grand Rapids, MI: Revell Books, 2006.

Periodicals

Nell Bernstein, "You Can't Be Anorexic—You're Black!" *Marie Claire*, December 2004, pp. 121–22.

Audrey D. Brashich, "Starving for Friendship: Can You Catch Anorexia from a Friend?" *Teen People*, October 1, 2004, p. 126.

Meaghan Buchan, "Understanding My Eating Disorder 10 Years Later," *Cosmopolitan*, January 2006, pp. 104–107.

Jill Meredith Collins, "Nurturing Destruction: Eating Disorders Online," *Off Our Backs*, November/December 2004, pp. 20–22.

Andrea Faiad, "Dying to Be Thin: Eating Disorders Are Ugly," *Current Health 2, a Weekly Reader Publication*, November 2006, pp. 20–23.

Cleo Glyde, "Failure to Lunch," *Marie Claire*, April 2007, pp. 115–17.

Diane Guernsey, "Eating Disorders," *Town & Country*, April 2006, pp. 177–81.

Lisa Ingrassia, "My Nine-Year Struggle with Anorexia by Brittany Snow," *People Weekly*, October 15, 2007, p. 89.

Ellyn Mantell, "Consumed By Guilt, I Just Stopped Eating," *Newsweek*, June 12, 2006, p. 20.

Roxanne Patel, "She Was Good at Losing Weight . . . Too Good," *Good Housekeeping*, July 2005, pp. 72–73.

Jill Percia, "I Was Anorexic," *CosmoGirl*, November 2006, pp. 94–95.

Lynn Santa Lucia, "Driven to Be Thin," *Scholastic Choices,* September 2006, pp. 20–26.

Jenni Schaefer, "The Lost Boys," *CosmoGirl*, May 2007, pp. 122–24.

Amanda Smith, "The Mirror Has Two Faces," *Dance Magazine*, July 2006, pp. 34–35.

Sora Song, "Starvation on the Web," *Time*, July 18, 2005, p. 57.

Ericka Souter, "Anorexia, Again," *People Weekly*, December 11, 2006, p. 95.

Polly Sparling, "Empty Inside: Eating Disorders Involve Much More than Wanting to Be Thin," *Current Health 2, a Weekly Reader Publication*, January 2005, pp. 19–20.

Rachael Swirsky, "Weighing Self-Worth," *Odyssey*, May 2004, pp. 45–47.

Michelle Tan, "My Triumph over Anorexia (Scarlett Pomers)," *People Weekly*, August 27, 2007, p. 91.

Jennifer Wulff, "Pressure to Be Perfect," *People Weekly*, July 26, 2004, p. 72.

Internet Sources

PBS *NOVA*, "Dying to Be Thin," December 2000. www.pbs.org/wgbh/nova/thin.

Grace Bowman, "Making Myself Eat," *Elle Magazine*, April 2006. www.gracebowman.net/ws.htm.

Debra Mittler, "I Was Starving to Death: A True Story on Anorexia," BellaOnline, 2007. www.bellaonline.com/ArticlesP/art44818.asp.

Peter Overton, "Deadly Seduction," *60 Minutes*, September 18, 2005. http://sixtyminutes.ninemsn.com.au/article.aspx?id=259339.

Peter Overton, "What a Waste," *60 Minutes*, October 31, 2004. http://sixtyminutes.prev01.ninemsn.com.au/article.aspx?id=259231.

Peg Tyre, "Fighting Anorexia: No One to Blame," *Newsweek*, December 5, 2005. www.newsweek.com/id/51592.

Kyffin Webb, "Anorexia from Control to Chaos," *WireTap Magazine*, February 5, 2002. www.wiretapmag.org/stories/12356.

Source Notes

Overview

1. National Institute of Mental Health, "Study Tracks Prevalence of Eating Disorders," *Science News*, February 9, 2007. www.nimh.nih.gov.
2. Stella Jones, "Inside Anorexia," TeenWire, June 6, 2007. www.teenwire.com.
3. Lori Gottlieb, *Stick Figure: A Diary of My Former Self*. New York: Simon & Schuster, 2000, p. 73.
4. National Institute of Mental Health, "Eating Disorders," 2007. www.nimh.nih.gov.
5. Quoted in Andree Dignon, Angela Beardsmore, Sean Spain, and Ann Kuan, "'Why I Won't Eat': Patient Testimony from 15 Anorexics Concerning the Causes of Their Disorder," *Journal of Health Psychology*, 2006, pp. 942–56.
6. Jessica Lyons, "Anorexia—the Most Deadly Mental Illness—Is Definitely Not Just About Looking Thin," *Monterey County Weekly*, January 20, 2005. www.montereycountyweekly.com.
7. Aimee Liu, *Gaining: The Truth About Life After Eating Disorders*. New York: Warner Books, 2007, p. xii.
8. Jones, "Inside Anorexia."
9. Lauren Sackey, "The Heavy Loss of Anorexia," *Detroit Fashion Pages*, December 4, 2007. http://detroitfashionpages.com.
10. Laura Penny, "Having Starved Myself of Life for So Long, I'm Now Ravenous for It," *The Oxford Student*, February 17, 2005. www.oxfordstudent.com.
11. Quoted in Lisa Ingrassia, "My Nine-Year Struggle with Anorexia by Brittany Snow," *People Weekly*, October 15, 2007, p. 89.
12. Quoted in Paula Rath, "Nearly Wiped Out," *The Honolulu Advertiser*, January 24, 2005. http://the.honoluluadvertiser.com.
13. Julia K. De Pree, *Body Story*. Athens: Ohio University Press, 2004, p. 4.
14. Mayo Clinic, "Anorexia Nervosa," June 13, 2006. www.mayoclinic.com.
15. Quoted in Peter Overton, "Deadly Seduction," *60 Minutes*, September 18, 2005. http://sixtyminutes.ninemsn.com.au.
16. Quoted in *Daily Mail*, "Eating Disorders Misunderstood by Doctors," February 5, 2007. www.dailymail.co.uk.
17. Harriet Brown, "Stigma of Anorexia Keeps Many from Help," *Wisconsin State Journal*, November 10, 2007, p. A8.
18. Quoted in Margarite Nathe, "A Deadly Dread of Food," *Endeavors Magazine*, Fall 2006. http://research.unc.edu.
19. Julie K. De Pree, *Body Story*, p. 4.

How Serious Is Anorexia?

20. Quoted in *Guardian Unlimited*, "'Everyone Knew She Was Ill. The Other Girls, the Model Agencies . . . Don't Believe It When They Say They Didn't,'" *The Observer Magazine*, January 14, 2007. http://observer.guardian.co.uk.
21. Steven Levenkron, *Anatomy of Anorexia*. New York/London: W.W. Norton & Company, 2000, p. 61.
22. Quoted in Jesse Fonner, "Students Face Eating Disorders," *The Stanford Daily*, June 6, 2001. http://daily.stanford.org.
23. Hilde Bruch, MD, *The Golden Cage: The Enigma of Anorexia Nervosa*. Cambridge, MA: Harvard University Press, 1978, p. vii.

24. Quoted in Peg Tyre, "Fighting Anorexia: No One to Blame," *Newsweek*, December 5, 2005. www.newsweek.com.

25. Quoted in Melinda Murphy, "Genetic Link to Anorexia?" CBS News, February 3, 2006. www.cbsnews.com.

26. Quoted in Denise Brodey, "Blacks Join the Eating Disorder Mainstream," *The New York Times*, September 20, 2005. www.nytimes.com.

27. Quoted in Christine Sams, "Anorexia Almost Killed Me: Daniel Johns," *Sydney Morning Herald*, June 6, 2004. www.smh.com.au.

28. Evelyn Strauss, "Facing the Plate," Salon, September 13, 2000. http://archive.salon.com.

29. Quoted in Overton, "Deadly Seduction."

30. Margaret Donlevy, "Anorexia Is Starving Our Little Angel of Life," *Edinburgh Evening News*, April 7, 2007. http://news.scotsman.com.

31. Quoted in PBS *NOVA*, "Dying to Be Thin," December 12, 2000. www.pbs.org.

32. Lauren Simmons (pseudonym), interview with author, January 5, 2008.

What Causes Anorexia?

33. Harriet Brown, "One Spoonful at a Time," *The New York Times*, November 26, 2006. www.nytimes.com.

34. Liu, *Gaining*, p. 41.

35. Levenkron, *Anatomy of Anorexia*, p. 43.

36. Dignon et al., "'Why I Won't Eat,'" pp. 942–56.

37. Dignon et al., "'Why I Won't Eat,'" pp. 942–56.

38. Quoted in PBS *NOVA*, "Dying to Be Thin."

39. Quoted in Nathe, "A Deadly Dread of Food."

40. Quoted in PBS *NOVA*, "Dying to Be Thin."

41. Quoted in Fran Yeoman, "Anorexia 'Cannot Be Picked Up by Looking at Photographs of Super-Thin Models,'" *The Times*, December 17, 2007. www.timesonline.co.uk.

42. Quoted in Denise Gellene, "Anorexia Is Linked to Prenatal Estrogen," *Los Angeles Times*, December 4, 2007. www.latimes.com.

43. Quoted in Kim Archer, "Eating-Disorder Study Suggests a Genetic Role," *Tulsa World*, February 20, 2007. www.tulsaworld.com.

44. Quoted in Jenni Schaefer, "The Lost Boys," *CosmoGirl*, May 2007, pp. 122–24.

45. Strauss, "Facing the Plate."

46. Quoted in PBS *NOVA*, "Dying to Be Thin."

What Are the Health Risks of Anorexia?

47. Bruch, *The Golden Cage*, p. 2.

48. Quoted in PBS *NOVA*, "Dying to Be Thin."

49. Quoted in PBS *NOVA*, "Dying to Be Thin."

50. Marcia Herrin and Nancy Matsumoto, "Medical Symptoms and Complications Associated with Anorexia," *The Parent's Guide to Eating Disorders*, July 2007. www.gurze.com.

51. Howard Markel, MD, "Cases: Anorexia Can Strike Boys Too," *The New York Times*, July 6, 2000. http://query.nytimes.com.

52. Quoted in Ron Hogan, "Marya Hornbacher," *Beatrice*, 1998. www.beatrice.com.

Can Anorexia Be Cured?

53. Debra Mittler, "I Was Starving to Death: A True Story on Anorexia," BellaOnline, 2007. www.bellaonline.com.

54. Levenkron, *Anatomy of Anorexia*, p. 199.

55. Quoted in Brown, "One Spoonful at a Time."

56. Tyre, "Fighting Anorexia: No One to Blame."

57. Mayo Clinic, "Anorexia Nervosa."

58. Quoted in Marcia Froelke Coburn, "When Girls Won't Eat," *Chicago Magazine*, March 2007. www.chicago mag.com.

59. Brown, "One Spoonful at a Time."

60. Brown, "One Spoonful at a Time."

61. Brown, "One Spoonful at a Time."

62. Quoted in Ginny Graves, "No Time to Lose," *Self*, June 2006, pp. 98–100.

63. Quoted in Graves, "No Time to Lose."

64. Laura Penny, "'Having Starved Myself of Life for So Long, I'm Now Ravenous for It,'" *The Oxford Student*, February 17, 2005. www.oxfordstudent.com.

List of Illustrations

How Serious Is Anorexia?

Anorexia Develops at a Young Age	31
Symptoms and Signs of Anorexia	32
Anorexia and Gender	33
The Disease of Delusion	34

What Causes Anorexia?

The Complex Causes of Anorexia	49
The Brain and Distorted Body Image	50
Body Mass Index	51
The Connection Between Anorexia and Emotional Disorders	52
Celebrity Anorexics	53

What Are the Health Risks of Anorexia?

Anorexia's Impact on the Body	66
Anorexia and Osteoporosis	67
Anorexia Destroys the Heart	68

Can Anorexia Be Cured?

Anorexia Treatment	82
How the Mandometer® Device Works	83
Anorexia: A Lasting Disease	84

Index

African Americans, increase in anorexia among, 22

age
  at onset of anorexia, 28, 31 (chart)
  of people with eating disorders, 21, 30
Alliance for Eating Disorder Awareness, 80
American Academy of Child & Adolescent Psychiatry, 79
American Journal of Psychiatry, 38
anemia, 57
  prevalence among anorexics, 65
anorexia
  ages affected by, 20–21
  average length of time battling, 84 (chart)
  causes of, 6, 10–11, 43–46
    controversy over, 35–36
  connection between emotional disorders and, 52 (chart)
  health risks of, 14–16, 54–60, 61 64, 66
  hormonal changes from, 57–58
  increase in, among young women, 31
  insidious nature of, 23
  prevalence of, 6, 9, 26, 30
  See also symptoms; treatment
anorexic(s)
  brain studies with, 37–38
  celebrity, 53 (table)
  characteristics of, 36–37, 48, 50
  lingering effects of malnutrition on, 59–60
  mothers
    health risks to children of, 67
    prenatal mortality and, 65
  percentage recieving treatment, 81
  resistance to treatment among, 69–70
  risks of weight gain in, 70–71
Archives of General Psychiatry (journal), 39

Bergh, Cecelia, 74, 75, 78

biological factors, role in development of anorexia, 49
Blumberg, Amy, 28
body dismorphic disorder (BDD), 50
body image, distorted, 11
  brain changes and, 50
body mass index (BMI), 51 (chart)
Bolton, Jim, 64
bones, effects of anorexia on, 55–56, 67
Bowman, Grace, 63
boys
  anorexia among, 9–10, 22–23
  anorexia-associated hormonal changes in, 7, 58
brain
  distorted body image and, 50
  effects of anorexia on, 58
  research on, with anorexics, 36–37
Brooks, Gayle, 21–22, 45
Brown, Diane, 17
Brown, Harriet, 8, 17, 35, 43, 73 74
Brown, Kitty, 73–74
Brown, Lauren, 17
Bruch, Hilde, 20, 54–55
Bulik, Cynthia, 18, 37, 44
bulimia nervosa, 6, 13–14
  percentage of anorexics developing, 30

Canada, increase in anorexia hospitalizations in, 83
Carpenter, Karen, 20
Carson, Kaelyn, 22
Centers for Disease Control and Prevention (CDC), 33
Cuzzolaro, Massimo, 78

Dawson, Dee, 21, 27
De Pree, Julia K., 14, 18, 46
deaths/mortality rate, 7, 20, 30
  among celebrity anorexics, 53 (table)
  from complications of anorexia, 65

by suicide, risk of among anorexics, 32
delusion, anorexia as disease of, 7, 34
depression, percentage of anorexics
    meeting criteria for, 48
DeVinny, Alex, 16
diabetes type 1, eating disorders among
    young women with, 48
*Diagnostic and Statistical Manual of Mental
    Disorders,* 20
Donlevy, Margaret, 23–24
Dying to be Thin (TV documentary), 37,
    55

Eastman, Lizzy, 79
electrolytes, 57
emotional disorders, connection between
    anorexia and, 52 (chart)
environment, role in development of
    anorexia, 39–40
Europe, treatment success rates in, 84

Flicker, Jacqui, 19
Frampton, Ian, 46

gender
    fear of being overweight and, 52
    incidence of anorexia and, 9–10, 30, 31,
        33 (chart)
genetics, role in development of anorexia,
    39
girls
    African American, increase in anorexia
        among, 22
    anorexia-associated hormonal changes
        in, 58
    models as role models for, 41
    percent seeing themselves as overweight,
        48
    prevalence of anorexia among, 10, 30
Glyde, Cleo, 9
*The Golden Cage: The Enigma of Anorexia
    Nervosa* (Bruch), 20
Goodman, Erika, 37, 55–56
Gottlieb, Lori, 9
Grefe, Lynn, 35
Guernsey, Diane, 62

Guerra, Concha, 45
Guisinger, Shan, 79

Hamilton, Linda, 55
heart, effects of anorexia on, 58–59, 61, 68
Herrin, Marcia, 58–59
Hodges, Carolyn, 71
Hornbacher, Marya, 11, 60, 62
Hornby, Leslie (Twiggy), 41
hospitalization
    cost of, 17, 71–72
    increase in among young women in
        Canada, 83

Japan, treatment seeking for anorexia in,
    34
Johns, Daniel, 22
Johnson, Charles, 40, 44
Johnson, Craig, 39, 40
Jones, Stella, 8–9
Jourdan, Thea, 43
Journal of Health Psychology, 37–38

Kaye, Walter H., 37–38, 47, 70–71
kidneys, effects of anorexia on, 58
Krantz, Mori J., 21

laxatives, use of, to lose weight, 33
le Grange, Daniel, 17, 35, 72
leucopenia, 57
    prevalence among anorexics, 65
Levenkron, Steven, 8, 20, 32, 36
Liu, Aimee, 11, 28, 36
Lyons, Jessica, 11, 62

malnourishment, 56–57
Mandometer method, 74–76, 83
    success rate of, 81
Markel, Howard, 54, 59
Matsumoto, Nancy, 58–59
Maudsley Approach, 72–73
media, role in increase in anorexia, 41–42,
    46
Mehler, Philip S., 21
menstruation, loss of, 7, 14, 58, 65
Mileski, Charlie, 9

Mittler, Debra, 69
models, average weight of, vs. average
    women, 52

National Association of Anorexia Nervosa
    and Associated Disorders, 20
    on prevalence of eating disorders among
        high school students, 33
National Eating Orders Association, 34
National Institutes of Mental Health
    (NIMH), 8, 9, 69, 70
    on anorexia among males, 10
    on conditions coexisting with anorexia,
        63
    on eating disorders as medical illnesses,
        27
    on prevalence of anorexia among
        females, 30
National Women's Health Information
    Center, 44

obsessive-compulsive disorder (OCD), 52
    (chart)
Odi, Nalani, 14
O'Farrell, Peggy, 29
osteopenia, 56
    prevalence among anorexics, 65
osteoporosis, 67
overweight, perception of being, among
    young girls, 48

pancytopenia, 57
Penny, Laura, 13, 76
perfectionism, as trait of anorexics, 36, 41,
    48
Pieken, Kennedy, 21
prenatal mortality, 65
pro-Ana Web sites, 16
Procopio, Marco, 39
psycho-developmental factors, role in
    development of anorexia, 49
puberty, age of onset among girls, risk of
    anorexia and, 52

refeeding syndrome, 70
Reston, Ana Carolina, 20, 58
Roberts, Bria, 23

Rosen, David S., 21, 29

Sawyer, Susan, 16
Schenk, Karen, 13
Sedden, Hannah, 54, 63
seizures, during refeeding, 65
self-mutilation, 24–25
serotonin, 37–38
Simmons, Laura, 24–25
Simon, Ilyse, 26
Snow, Brittany, 13, 45
sociocultural factors, role in development
    of anorexia, 41–42, 49
Strauss, Evelyn, 41
Striegel-Moore, Ruth, 42
substance abuse, among anorexics, 33
suicide
    attempts by anorexics, 83
    risk of death from, among anorexics, 32
symptoms, 6, 32, 54
    behavioral, 12
    physical, 12–13

Taylor, Kate, 46
Thornton, Chris, 80
treatment, 7
    challenges in, 71–72
    cost of, 17, 71–72, 81
    difficulty of, 16–17
    family-centered, 72–73
    Mandometer method, 74–76
    percent of anorexics receiving, 81
    phases of, 70, 82
    resistance to, 69–70
    success rates, in Europe, 84
Twiggy (Leslie Hornby), 41
Tyre, Peg, 19, 71

Wallmeyer, Clare, 56, 61
Webb, Kyffin, 64, 77
Web sites, pro-Ana, 16
weight gain, during treatment, 81
Williams, Alex, 28
Wolfe, Barbara, 80
Women Today (magazine), 13

Yonker, Theresa, 29

About the Author

Peggy J. Parks holds a BS degree from Aquinas College in Grand Rapids, Michigan, where she graduated magna cum laude. She is an author who has written more than 60 nonfiction educational books for children and young adults, as well as self-publishing her own cookbook called *Welcome Home: Recipes, Memories, and Traditions from the Heart.* Parks lives in Muskegon, Michigan, a town that she says inspires her writing because of its location on the shores of Lake Michigan.